Writing Memoir

Writing
MEMOIR

The Practical Guide to Writing and
Publishing the Story of Your Life

Jerry Payne

Faydelis Press

Writing Memoir

The Practical Guide to Writing and Publishing the Story of Your Life

Jerry Payne

FIRST EDITION

ISBN: 978-0-9835814-8-2
eBook ISBN: 978-0-9835814-9-9

Library of Congress Control Number: 2016911435

Cover Design: Karen Major, LivingTOOgood.com.
(Thanks, Karen!)

To my son. May the story of your life be a magical one.

Contents

"Each time someone dies, a library burns."

—JANDY NELSON

Introduction

I'm a ghostwriter. That means I write for other people. (Not everyone knows this. Once, a cab driver in Key West, hearing what I did for a living, excitedly told me that I'd come to the right place because "we've got *lots* of great ghost stories in this town!") In my career, I've written or edited various business how-to books, medical books, diet and nutrition books, geopolitical books, a gardening book, a book on sunken treasure, and a book on how to quit smoking. Mostly, however, I've written memoirs. I wrote one not long after I started my ghostwriting career and was so drawn to the experience, I soon found myself focusing on them.

Memoirs are special. As I'll discuss in this book, and as you'll discover in the process of writing your memoir, there is something profoundly revelatory in exploring a life to the depth that's required to write about it. I'll make a case in the very first chapter that any honest memoir does just this. A memoir is an exploration. And each memoir I've worked on has been illuminating in its own unique way. I suppose that's not surprising; every memoir is unique because every life is unique.

It's the exploration that's the key. We'll talk about the objectivity and self-awareness true exploration requires. Good memoirs help generate self-awareness, which, in turn, makes good memoirs. Poor memoirs lack this quality. Poor memoirs are often superficial and self-absorbed and egotistical. Unfortunately, there are too many of this kind of memoir. "Here, let me tell you how interesting I am." No, thanks. If that's your idea of a memoir, you're probably not going to get much out of this book. A good memoir won't be about you. It'll be about your reader. That's what exploration does. It uncovers that which links us to the human condition. This book is about that link and, therefore, about your connection to the reader.

A good bit of that connection depends on your quality of writing, and so I should say this before we go any further: you're going to learn a lot in this book (hopefully!) about *writing* a memoir, but the one thing I can't teach is *how to write*. My belief is that nobody can teach you this. You can learn how to improve your writing. You can learn some things about sentence structure and syntax and organization and plot development and character description and other parts of the writing process (all of which you'll find here) so as to better hone your craft. But something of the craft has to be there to begin with.

It was the philosophy of Mr. Reichenfeld, my violin teacher in fourth grade. If you wanted Mr. Reichenfeld to teach you to play an instrument, you had to pass a test. He'd sit you down beside him at a piano and he'd hit a key. You then had to sing that key. If he hit middle C, you had to sing middle C. You could either do it or you couldn't. And if you couldn't, he'd apologize but say the violin wasn't for you, and that was that. His reasoning was simple: if you had no ear for music, how could you properly play it?

I believe it's the same with writing. There's a certain natural ability that you simply must possess to be a writer, and nobody can give that ability to you. If you don't have an "ear" for good writing, you're not going to be able to create it. Of course, having an ear for it doesn't guarantee that you'll excel at it. I passed Mr. Reichenfeld's test, but I quickly discovered that I wasn't cut out to be a violinist. My lessons stopped after one year (much to the relief of everyone in the household who'd been subjected to my evening practice sessions).

My guess is that if you've come this far, that is to say you at least picked up a book on how to write your own memoir, you probably know you have a minimum of *some* talent for putting words together. But you also know you could use a little help. That's a good spot to be in: confident enough to take the leap but not cocky to where you can't imagine that anybody could teach you something you don't already know. You'll do just fine.

In summary, all I ask is the capacity to explore your life honestly and a minimum amount of wordsmithing ability. With those prerequisites, you're all set to learn how to write an extraordinary memoir.

One housekeeping note: I use several examples here from books I have ghostwritten, but confidentiality is an important part of my particular trade, one I take very seriously. It's the code of the ghostwriter. Therefore, except for the examples where specific permission has been granted for me to excerpt my clients' work, the examples have been altered from their published text and, in some cases, rewritten significantly. Occasionally, I've also purposely fudged the details regarding from which book and from whom the example has come. I trust that's understandable. It's the point of the example in question that's important, after all, not the source. This might seem like a minor matter, but I talk in here about an implied "contract" you're going to have with your readers regarding factuality. What kind of teacher would I be if I didn't hold myself to the same standards I advise?

Okay. With that out of the way, let's start about this business of writing the story of your life.

CHAPTER ONE

A Good Reason to Write

"Writing is easy. All you do is sit down
at a typewriter and open a vein."

—RED SMITH

People have all manner of reasons for writing a memoir. If you've picked up this book, you probably already have your own reasons. Far be it from me to second-guess them. Maybe you're writing your memoirs because you want some record of your life to survive you after death, a lasting mark that you were here, something your grandkids and potentially great-great-grandkids might one day read. That's a good reason. Maybe you're writing your memoirs because, over the years, you've learned some very important things about life that you believe others might be able to benefit from hearing, lessons you learned the hard way. You've overcome huge obstacles. Or mistakes. Maybe you have a story of inspiration to share. That's a good reason, too.

Or maybe you *haven't* overcome, and therein lies your story. Yours is a cautionary tale. Maybe you're writing because you're trying to make sense of a tragedy. Or maybe you just feel like your life would make more sense somehow if you saw it in print. (Remember the old Eagles song "James Dean"? Dean is imagined as believing that his life would "look all right" if he could just "see it on the silver screen.")

Maybe by revealing the story of your life, you'll get some publicity that'll be good for your business. It's an advertisement of sorts. Maybe you're retired and you just want a nice, neat collection of all the successes (and failures?) from your long and storied career. Maybe your story can help advance a social or political cause that's important to you. Maybe you've lived a life you know others are intensely curious about—that of a combat veteran, leader of an outlaw motorcycle gang, circus performer, porn star, drug addict, sports celebrity. Maybe you feel the need to tell your side of a story that someone else has publicly characterized wrongly, maybe even egregiously so.

Maybe you just want people to understand you better.

Maybe you want to understand yourself better.

These are all legitimate reasons, and while ghostwriting two dozen or so memoirs, I've heard every one of these and more. But that last one...that might be the best reason of all. *Maybe you want to understand yourself better.* "We do not write in order to be understood," the English poet Cecil Day-Lewis once said. "We write in order to understand." No matter what reason you have for writing your memoir, I'll guarantee one thing: if you write honestly, if you really plumb the depths of your own story, if you seek to tell the account of your life (or some part of your life) as objectively as you can, you're going to learn something about yourself in the process. Something you never knew before.

Know thyself, goes the ancient proverb, and I don't know of a better way to accomplish that than by examining one's life with the level of objectivity that's required to write an honest memoir. This, of course, assumes an honest memoir is the kind of memoir you want to write. Are there other kinds? I imagine a lot of memoirs have been written that weren't honest. Some were probably written that way intentionally, and some were probably written that way unintentionally. I'm not referring here, of course, to the minor details. We'll talk in the next chapter about how memory can sometimes fail us (her dress was really blue even though you can swear it was red), or about how it's okay (sometimes) to fudge a minor point, or how sometimes you might have to conjure up some dialogue that may not be how it went down word-for-word. There's a lot of this that's unavoidable. Rather, the kind of dishonesty I'm referring to here is the kind of dishonesty where the memoirist ends up portraying him or herself as a different person than he or she is. We're not talking about fudging the details. We're talking about fudging the main character.

There's a word for a book like that, and that word is *fiction*. Fiction is a fine thing to write, but fiction is not memoir. Fiction is fiction. *Memoir* is memoir. We're not writing novels here. To characterize your piece of fiction as true does a disservice to the reader, and it doesn't do you any good, either. Memoirs often live and die on their level of authenticity. There's just something about disingenuous writing that people can see through. It's hard to mislead or pull off embellishment or produce outright fakery over the course of an entire book. And the moment the reader senses the memoirist isn't being sincere, the memoirist loses the reader.

In truth, most cases of insincere memoir writing come about unintentionally. Yes, there are memoirs where the author purposely exaggerated the events of his or her life to portray a "better" or more "interesting" person, but most cases of disingenuous writing come about simply because the memoirist hasn't dug deep enough, hasn't examined thoroughly her motivations, perhaps, or the consequences of her actions. The result is, at best, a superficial story; at worst, a phony one. This is often what happens when writers lack a certain level of self-awareness. It's not a memoir; in fact, it's a piece of fiction, but if you want to see this phenomenon of self-*un*awareness in action, I can't think of a better example than the classic short story *The Golden Honeymoon* by Ring Lardner. (Get yourself a copy of this wonderful story and read it before you write so much as the first sentence of your memoir.)

This, of course, brings us back to the idea of understanding, of knowing thyself. Here's where it gets interesting. Writing an honest memoir requires self-awareness, and self-awareness is often the result of writing an honest memoir. It might seem like a catch-22, but it's not. The writing feeds off the honesty, and the honesty, in turn, feeds off the writing. It's a beautiful symbiosis. And it is in that symbiosis that you can learn something about yourself, something important, something you never knew before. I've never had a single client who, somewhere along the course of writing his or her memoir, didn't have at least one *aha!* moment. Something epiphanic always occurs. Something hidden becomes revealed. Always. And I would submit that it is in that *aha!* moment (or *aha!* moment*s*) that you have every reason you ever need to write a memoir. Trust me on this.

Here's an example. I once had a client who overcame a severe weight problem. The book started out as a motivational memoir, centering on how "Tom" lost over two-hundred pounds. Kind of a "you can do it, too" book. It was meant to be inspirational but also practical. There was a lot of technical stuff about diet and exercise and good nutrition. But a strange thing happened along the way. During the course of writing a couple of chapters about Tom's background—his childhood and his adolescence, the times in his life when he really started putting all the weight on that he would eventually lose—Tom started picking up on some psychological patterns. He began connecting some dots that led him to better understand why he ultimately headed toward obesity in the first place. These discoveries also helped him realize that today, even with all he knows about exercise and nutrition, he still often struggles to keep his eating, and therefore weight, under control. Tom took a break from the book and during this time, he sought some professional analysis that helped him see the very root of his weight problem. Delving into his underlying issues wasn't easy. But the result, about a year or so later, was a more self-aware person, and, once we picked up the project again, a much different, and infinitely better, book.

Your epiphany might not be as life changing. It may, in fact, be small in the grand scheme of your life. That's okay. It will still be worthwhile. And achieving it obviously doesn't make the other reasons for writing a memoir invalid. Heck, they may even be better for their respective purposes. Having something your great-great-grandkids may someday want to read is a good enough reason in and of itself. Same goes for writing something that helps your business or summarizes your career or helps your cause. Whatever your motivation is, so long as it's honest, it's good enough as far as I'm concerned. You'll never catch me trying to talk someone *out* of writing. But know that there's another reason out there, too, and you may not even grasp its significance until you've finished your book. In the end, no matter your motivations, you're going to be glad you wrote your book because of what you learned about yourself in the process.

Okay, so maybe there is *one* reason I would question, that would cause me to, in fact, try to talk you out of writing. If you're looking to write a memoir because you think your book can be the next great bestseller, the next *Wild* or *Tuesdays with Morrie* or *The Liars' Club*, I would recommend that you reconsider. If you think you're going to become wealthy with your book, if you're thinking Oprah's Book Club, or if you have visions of attending the Hollywood premier of the film version of your book, I would tell you to please come back down to earth. We're going to discuss publishing later. Suffice it to say for now, that the odds of any of these things happening are slim to the point where you'd probably be better off playing the lottery. I know, I know—but *your* book is different. Your book is certain to be a bestseller. Believe me, I've seen enough great books get passed over, and I know enough about the economics and vagaries of the publishing industry to almost guarantee that your book will not make you: a) wealthy, or b) a household name. Sorry. That's just the way it is.

This doesn't mean you can't get published (or make profit on your self-published book); it just means you have to be more realistic, and, hopefully, you've got a different set of motivations than writing for the potential fame and money. If you don't have a different set of motivations, may I at least offer the one where you have the opportunity to learn about yourself?

With all that said, with your bubble hopefully not burst beyond repair (and maybe even your level of intrigue a little higher with all this talk about epiphanies and understanding), let's now look a bit closer into this idea of writing an honest book.

CHAPTER TWO

Your Contract with the Reader, Your Contract with Yourself

"A writer's job is to tell the truth."

—ERNEST HEMINGWAY

If you're going to write an honest memoir, maybe we should start by defining what a memoir is. And what it isn't. As you may guess, the word has a lot to do with the word memory. In fact, it comes to us from the Anglo-French *mémorie*, meaning memory or remembrance. You often see it or hear it pluralized ("memoirs") when the writer or speaker ought to have used the singular tense ("memoir"). Not that a person's memoir won't include a ton of individual memories, but the plural typically refers to enough memories to recall a person's entire life, all (or most) of their memories. There's another word for that kind of book and it's *autobiography*. You often hear about a retired general or politician or sports hero or business magnate writing his or her "memoirs." What they're doing is writing their life story, their autobiography.

In this case, we typically start by reading about the writer's childhood and siblings and parents. Sometimes we even go back beyond that, to their parents' lives and their grandparents' lives and even where their ancestors were from. We read about the writer's schooling and home life and then about his young adulthood and his early influences. Then we read about his career: high points, low points, successes, failures, and all the moments in between. And we read about everything else, even up until the writing of the book itself! If you're thinking about writing your "memoirs," your autobiography, that's okay. If you're looking to make a record of your life for posterity, go for it. As you'll see, we'll be more concerned here with "memoir" than "memoirs," but the same ideas apply. They just apply over and over again. A memoir plus a memoir plus a memoir (plus however many more) equals memoirs. Told well, each memoir is a story unto itself. There should be an overall storyline (your life) with continuity, but any given memoir therein ought to be able to stand on its own.

So what does it mean to write "a" memoir? A memoir centers on a significant part, or time, of your life. Think of it as an episode of your life. It could be the twelve years you spent in Paris or the single day you spent kidnapped by a serial rapist. Either way, to tell the story, you might need to draw on background information from your life that's outside the main timeframe. You might need to provide some details about your childhood or your job, or why you decided to go to Paris to begin with, but, even then, the emphasis is still on the major event on which your story is centered.

A memoir could also be centered on a significant *aspect* of yourself over time, maybe even a long time. Perhaps it's your willingness to risk death and your memoir details the dozen or so mountain-climbing expeditions you've been on. Or maybe it's about your career as a football coach or speech therapist. Or about your life as a blind person or a person living with OCD. It's not autobiography, because it's more about a part of your life rather than your whole life, even if that part has been around as long as you have. But whether it's a part of your life, a certain time period in your life, or an aspect of who you are, that's a memoir. That's the story.

As discussed in Chapter One, the first and best thing you can do with your memoir is to make it honest, to make it genuine. This seems easy on the surface, but notice that in our talk about what a memoir is, words like "episode" and "story" were used. These are the kind of words we often associate with fiction. But if we're going to write a compelling memoir, we need to start associating these words with nonfiction, too. As we'll see, memoir is kin to the novel. There's nothing wrong with relating a true event in the same manner in which you'd relate an invented story. In fact, there's everything right about it.

These days, telling a true tale in a creative, interesting, literary way—telling it like a story, in other words—has become known as "creative nonfiction." This little phrase came into being sometime in the last half century, but, in truth, people have been telling true tales creatively since humans first put pen to paper (or stylus to papyrus), and even back before that when stories were only passed along orally. But it's a useful description, serving to help us separate "story" type nonfiction (like the memoir) from other nonfiction like journalism, or technical or academic writing. Think of your history textbook from high school. True content? Sure. Creatively told? Probably not so much.

We'll talk about the structure of a story, and therefore the structure of a good memoir, in Chapter Four. For now, it's important to consider that your memoir, to be interesting and compelling and even edge-of-your-seat page-turning, needs to be more than just a dry recitation of facts and dates. Ah, but here's where things get a little dicey. If we're not careful, this idea can seem like a license to embellish or even misrepresent, or even outright fabricate. Not that you would consciously seek to do any of these things (at least I hope not). The problem often comes when you're genuinely trying to make things just a tad more interesting and you, ever so slightly, perhaps even unconsciously, take a liberty or two.

In editing a client's book once, I came across a passage about the day her husband walked out on her. It was a decent passage, but I told her I thought it needed to be beefed up a little more, starting with developing a bit more description. Nothing major, I said. But let's do a better job of setting the scene. Was it daytime? Night? What was it like outside? We needed a little something to add a little realism, to allow the reader a way to feel as though she were there, too. A fly on the wall. "Ooh, good idea," my client said. "Let's just say it was cold and raining. That'll set a more somber mood." Well, *was* it raining? "Oh, no," she said. "It was a beautifully sunny day."

Now, my client didn't want to purposely mislead the reader. She wasn't trying to be dishonest. She was being sincere in so far as she just wanted the reader to sense the gloomy set of circumstances. Her intentions were in the right place, and, at first blush, this doesn't seem like a very big literary sin. One might even think of it as a literary "technique." A cold, rainy day could serve to be almost metaphorical. But once we start fictionalizing nonfiction, we find ourselves on a slippery slope. Where does it end? Just with the weather? Or can we add the idea that there was a blackout at the time and the house was lit with one lonely candle that softly flickered out from the melancholy breeze wafting in from the open door the husband just walked out of, leaving us, finally and tragically, alone and in the dark? That sets an even better tone! The only problem is, it didn't happen that way. Our attempt at creative nonfiction has veered into fiction. Our true memoir has become a false narrative.

I assured her we could set a somber tone even with a beautifully sunny day. In fact, what we did was use the sunny day in an ironic sense. We played up the juxtaposition of the weather with the situation. Her husband walked out while outside, in the sunlit trees, birds sang without a care in the world. The irony highlighted the tragedy in her life.

The scene worked and we didn't need to fudge the facts. And it was a good thing because, later, I realized the scene took place in June. In Phoenix. It doesn't rain much in June in Phoenix, and it's certainly not very cold. All it takes is a couple of slips like that to lose credibility with the reader. And that's a hard thing to win back.

Whether you realize it or not, you have an agreement with the reader. An implied contract. Since you're presenting your book as a memoir, the reader presumes (rightfully so) that the material therein is true and factually accurate. If you breach that contract, if you violate the trust of your reader, why should he or she continue reading? How can you expect your reading audience to stick around? Why should they care about how your book turns out if you've given them reason to mistrust you? Part of the appeal, after all, was that your story was supposed to be a true one. If the reader wanted fiction, he or she would have picked up a novel.

Now, this doesn't mean the reader expects perfect recall. We don't go through life recording everything that happens to us as it's happening. There's no way you can remember every detail from events that occurred in your life several years ago, or even several days ago. Or even yesterday. And that's part of our implied contract, too. There's an asterisk next to the clause that says, "the material within this book is true and factually accurate," and that asterisk leads to a note that reads: *to the best of the writer's recollection.* That's all the reasonable reader expects. If my client above didn't remember the weather, I would have suggested we leave it out and build the mood in another way. Because she remembered it as sunny, we used that. To create a cold and rainy day from thin air would have been misleading and a breach of our contract with the reader.

Within the bounds of your best recollection, there's some latitude. For the most part, it's enough to believe that it *probably* happened this or that way, or that some event *seems likely* to have occurred as you described it from your memory. This idea is most noticeable with dialogue. Who can remember a conversation verbatim, even one you just had this morning with your neighbor? But we can certainly write the dialogue, based on our memory, of the overall *gist* of the conversation: *Bob turned white and exclaimed, "But I thought you were dead!"* Maybe Bob actually exclaimed, "But you're dead!" or "But how can you be alive?" or "You're alive?! No way!" As we have no audio recording of what Bob actually said, it's okay to create the dialogue in a way that conveys the gist of it as you best recall it. So long as you're not messing with the facts in a material way, you're fine. The reader understands.

It's the same with most minor details. If you honestly believe, to the best of your recollection, that she was wearing a red dress when she walked into the room, does it matter if it was, in fact, blue? Probably not. But check the context just to be sure. Would it make a difference? That's your test. If we find out two chapters later the police believe the murder was committed by a woman in a blue dress, then it might matter a great deal what color dress you saw her wearing that night. But if it's just a descriptive detail you're using to help create an image for the reader, then who really cares? Who's going to call you on it or feel as if they've somehow been slighted?

Just the same, it never hurts to get corroboration. If the incident was twenty years ago and you're a little fuzzy on the facts, maybe there's somebody you can consult with who was there. A witness. Maybe a phone call to your cousin, who was the one who opened the door that night to let her in, can confirm that, yes, the dress was indeed red, and not only that, it was strapless. Not that your cousin's recollection is necessarily any better than yours, but at least you now have a second opinion.

There are times you may want to change a name or a place just to protect someone's privacy, or, from a legal standpoint, maybe even to protect your own backside (we'll discuss legalities in greater detail later). I once wrote a memoir for a client where we had to fictionalize a whole town and use pseudonyms for an entire family. These people could have been in actual danger had their identities been revealed. There's nothing wrong with a little fudging in a case like this, but in keeping with our implied contract, you might want to consider a note at the front of the book. We used this one: "The story that follows is true. Names of some people and certain places have been changed." With this stipulation in place, we were a little more free to fudge. We adjusted the readers' expectations up front. Nevertheless, they still expected a true story (and they got one).

So much for honesty about material facts. As we discussed in the last chapter, there's another type of honesty in writing memoir that goes beyond the details. Yes, you have to be honest with your reader, but you also have to be honest with yourself. This was the upshot of Chapter One, where we discussed why this kind of honesty is good for *you*. Now let's discuss why this kind of honesty is good for the reader, too.

You see, what a reader often looks for in a memoir (consciously or unconsciously, maybe more the latter as most readers would probably tell you they're just looking for something good to read) is a lesson or a message—something he or she can relate to, maybe not in the details (maybe they've never spent twelve years in Paris or spent a day with a serial rapist), but somewhere in the general themes that collectively make up the human condition. You've gone through something. Maybe it's something life-altering, maybe it's something frightening, maybe it's just a period of many years or a series of many changes. But a simple retelling only gives the reader one dimension of the story. How did this "something" affect you? How did it make you feel? How does it make you feel now? What did you learn from it? The answers to these questions are what humanize the memoir. It's the answers that take the memoir from a simple narrative to a story of human interest. This is what it means to "get something" out of a book. Conversely, it's what's missing when someone finishes a book and says, "Well, it was okay, but I really just didn't *get* anything out of it."

I have learned that, surprisingly, the answers to questions about how some incident made the memoirist feel or what he or she learned aren't always apparent when one sets out to write his or her memoir. Heck, the *questions* may not even be apparent. These are the self-discoveries that writing a memoir makes possible (and worthwhile), and it is here where honesty and self-awareness are most needed.

Want to dig down to get to the real truth of your story? Want to generate some self-awareness as you're writing your book? Let me give you two magical words to remember: *how* and *why*. How did that incident really come about? Why did you act a certain way? Why did you react the way you did? How did it make you feel? Why did you move? Leave her? Quit that job? Why did you feel sad or happy or relieved or lost? How were you able to move forward? Every time you come to a pivotal moment in your book (your life), ask yourself how and why. The what and the when and the who are easy. Those are the facts. The how and the why are the story.

I've often said that when I help someone write a memoir, I'm part ghostwriter-editor and part Dr. Phil. My "why" and "how" questions help the client tell the real story, the story behind the story, if you will. It's what a good therapist does. I know I've tried more than a few clients' patience with my lines of questioning (one of them actually said, "What are you, writing a book?"), but the end results have been truer, more genuine books. To learn about yourself, you need to learn about your motivations. That fleshes you out more fully, making the main character in the book (you!) infinitely more interesting. Who wants to read a story about the life of a shallow person blundering along with no self-awareness, and therefore no ability to reflect, and, therefore, no lessons to impart?

Be warned: this isn't always easy. Self-discovery can be painful. You might learn something about yourself you don't like, something you'd like to change. Something you *need* to change, which might require a lot of effort. Or, in the process of digging deep into your past, you might have to relive moments you'd rather forget or, in fact, have long forgotten. Contemplating how you felt about a tragedy, for instance, might mean having to open an old wound. Thinking through a failed marriage might mean having to reconsider a period in your life that you thought you'd left in the past. It's a scary thing. But it's the digging deep that will allow you to learn more about *you* and therefore allow you to write a deeper, more genuine, *better* book. And this is what the reader is looking for.

The lessons you've learned along the way don't need to be expressly spelled out, by the way. Readers aren't stupid. They don't need to be beaten over the head with some "moral" of the story. What they need is your reaction and your response to what happened to you. They need to see how it affected you and what you did with the hard knocks. They'll relate to the lesson by seeing how you related to it. At best, maybe it's something that fits into their own lives somewhere. At worst, they get to see life from a different perspective, one they'd never considered before. Either way, the reader grows a little on the coattails of your honesty.

You owe it to yourself to be honest and to dig deep. But there's an implied contract with the reader as well. You owe your reader truth in the details (to the best of your recollection) and truth in the big picture, too. You owe it to your reader to fully flesh out the complex, fascinating, human character that is you.

CHAPTER THREE

Learning from the Masters

*"The greatest part of a writer's time is spent
in reading, in order to write; a man will turn
over half a library to make one book."*

—SAMUEL JOHNSON

If you were just starting to learn golf, how would you go about it? Would you just grab a set of clubs, get out on the golf course, and start whacking golf balls? Probably not. If you were smart, you'd take a lesson or two. At the least, you might decide to look around and take note of how experienced golfers play the game. You might try to emulate the stance and swing of a professional. You'd watch, and you'd learn.

And yet, time and again, I see would-be writers start out by just tapping away at a keyboard, with no direction and no clue as to how others before them did it. Look, if you're going to write a memoir, aren't you at least curious as to how successful, best-selling memoirists wrote *their* books? Don't you think you might be able to pick up *something* useful? I sometimes have young people, contemplating an eventual career in writing, ask me for advice on how to get started. It's tempting to say, "Just write!" but I give what I think is better advice: *read*. Become a student of the game in other words. Look at what the experts have done. To write great literature, read great literature. If you want to write a great memoir, read great memoirs. I think doing so is nothing less than a necessity for anybody seriously interested in writing the best book he or she can write. If I had to point to the one thing that has been most helpful to me in my career, it's been this, far and above anything else.

With this advice in mind, before we even get into any of the more "practical" and specific instructions for how to write a great memoir, let's go big picture and see just what, from the writings of the masters, we might be able to learn about the genre. Let me share with you some of my all-time favorite memoirs, some of the best, some of the books that have moved me, made me go "wow!" as I read them, or just plain made me want to become a better writer.

The Liars' Club by Mary Karr. As far as I'm concerned, this is the gold standard. Read this one if you don't have time to read any of the others listed here. (But find a way to make time for them anyway!) First released in 1995, this book about Karr's childhood in a dysfunctional family single-handedly ushered in a wave of confessional memoirs, none of which could match it in humor or poignancy.

This Boy's Life by Tobias Wolff. It was Wolff who (thankfully) advised Karr to write a story about her childhood. He certainly knew something about the process, having written about his own childhood in this book, first released in 1989. Like any good memoir, Wolff relates his story in such a way that, although the details might not be familiar to us, the universality of his themes (in his case, his boyhood) makes it resonate nonetheless.

A Moveable Feast by Ernest Hemingway. Hey, not every memoir has to be about childhood. This memoir, published in 1964, details Hemingway's time in Paris in the 1920s as he was just starting his career. Hemingway does something remarkable with this book: he makes you want to somehow walk into the pages and live those times with him. You wish you could go back in time (Owen Wilson's character does just this in the film *Midnight in Paris*) and rub shoulders with "Hem" and his friends F. Scott Fitzgerald, Gertrude Stein, Ezra Pound, and others. Hemingway (my all-time favorite writer) wrote simply but powerfully.

Speaking of Gertrude Stein, *The Autobiography of Alice B. Toklas* is a greatly illustrative example of true creativity in memoir writing. I don't recommend writers take chances like this one, but for Stein, it worked. (Hemingway called it "a damned pitiful book," but he was always a better writer than a critic.) First released in 1933 in the guise of an autobiography of her long-time companion (Alice), the book is really a memoir about Stein told in a kind of second-hand way. It's brilliant, and exceptionally entertaining.

Darkness Visible by William Styron. First released in 1990, this memoir of Styron's struggle with suicidal depression (the subtitle is *A Memoir of Madness*) is the perfect example of a memoir about one particular thing, or time, in a person's life. This book is not Styron's memoirs. This is *a* memoir. It's extraordinarily focused, as evidenced by its brevity. At only eighty-six pages, it's also a fine example of how memoirs don't have to be long, rambling reminiscences with never-ending description and suffocating detail. Read this if you want to grasp the beauty of a powerful story compactly told.

The Year of Magical Thinking by Joan Didion is another example of a book centered on a singular event or set of circumstances. Released in 2005, the memoir recounts the year in Didion's life following her husband's sudden death. Like all honest memoirs (the best kind), it's an intimate portrait, intensely personal, thereby helping to make it the powerful and moving book that it is.

Wild by Cheryl Strayed. A great memoir carries a distinctive voice, notably the voice of the memoirist (even Stein's *Autobiography* did this, though it was ostensibly Alice's book). Strayed's 2012 release reveals a unique personality through her writing, so real that you feel as though you know her well by the end of the book, like you just took a journey with a friend. Good quality in a memoir, that.

Other classic memoirs I recommend: *Good-bye to All That* by Robert Graves, *Girl Interrupted* by Susanna Kaysen, *Black Boy* by Richard Wright, *The Crack-Up* by F. Scott Fitzgerald, *Speak, Memory* by Vladimir Nabakov, and probably about a hundred other ones. Make your own list. Search online. But don't spend too much time agonizing over which memoirs to read. Just pick one. When you finish it, pick another one.

Read memoirs that don't seem to have anything to do with you. Stretch yourself. Take a walk down a road you've never been on. I've never struggled with clinical depression, but I found Styron's book fascinating. I'm not black, but Wright's account of his life in the Jim Crow south was extremely compelling to me.

Great memoirs transcend time and circumstance, and they do so because of their universality of themes. What all these books have in common is that they give us a glimpse into the human condition. When you read a memoir that takes you out of your familiar day-to-day life, that takes you out of your comfort zone, you can see how the writer is able to provide this glimpse. The greats, no matter how different they may be from you, or how different their circumstances, or how separated you may be even from the times in which they lived, nevertheless make it seem as though they're talking directly to *you*. Their writing is sincere, personal, often witty, and, above all else, they never seem to be trying too hard. It's no coincidence that these are many of the same qualities we like in our friends.

One of the key characteristics you'll find in the works of the masters is their faithful adherence to Anton Chekhov's famous admonition: *show, don't tell*. Chekhov wrote, "Don't tell me the moon is shining. Show me the glint of light on broken glass." This "show, don't tell" idea is a mainstay of any basic writing course for a reason. Showing instead of telling incites the reader's imagination, and this is the job of the memoir writer. Telling lays it all out there, leaving nothing to be imagined. The reader's mind only has to work on a very basic level. She's reading words. But when the reader is shown, when a picture is painted, the reader can imagine. A lot more of the mind is used. The reader becomes mentally (even emotionally) *involved*.

Here, this is what I mean: Mary Karr in *The Liars' Club* writes not of a big-city department store that intimidates her as a child from a small town and a poverty-stricken family. She writes of a "vast and canyonlike" department store where the "metal escalators meandered between floors and threatened to eat my toes off at the end." In *Good-bye to All That*, Robert Graves, writing about his time in the trenches in World War I, doesn't just say that bullets striking the barbed wire made distinct noises and flew in unpredictable directions. He instead writes that the barbed wire "turned them and sent them spinning in a head-over-heels motion—ping! rockety-ockety-ockety-ockety into the woods behind." Hemingway, in *A Moveable Feast*, doesn't speak of autumn coming to Paris. He speaks of rain and how "the cold wind would strip the leaves from the trees in the Place Contrescarpe."

In each case, as readers, we become more involved in the scene, more a part of it. We hear or see or feel what the writer heard or saw or felt. And it becomes that much more real to us, that much more powerful.

Like most things in life, however, moderation is the key. Beginning writers, eager to heed Chekhov's advice, often have a tendency to overdo it, painting the picture with every color on their palette. They throw in multiple adjectives when a single one would do, or perhaps where none is needed at all. A sentence I actually read somewhere: *Josh slipped on the frozen ice.* Is "frozen" really necessary to modify "ice"? Obviously, the writer was trying to better describe the scene, trying to show and not tell. His heart was in the right place, but his execution failed. Maybe there's a better way to describe the ice or to describe the slipping action. Or maybe, in this case, it would be sufficient to just say "Josh slipped on the ice."

Sometimes, in addition to adding redundancy, too much flowery description serves to just plain bog things down. *Kevin, trembling, his cold, frosted mug shaking in his quivering hand, was warily inspecting the other patrons of the dark, dim bar, nervously eyeing them with fearful apprehension.* Notice how far this writer has gone to show instead of just tell us that Kevin was nervous. One has to applaud the effort, I suppose, but we probably grasped the idea with "trembling." Was it necessary to pile on the words "shaking," "quivering," "warily," "nervously," "fearful," and "apprehension"? Furthermore, was it necessary to tell us the mug was cold *and* frosted? Was it necessary to even describe the mug in the first place? Did we need to know the bar was both dark and dim?

Not everything needs to be described in detail, and not every scene needs to be painted. Even Chekhov would admit that sometimes it's okay to just *tell.* Much depends on the context. We'll revisit description in a later chapter.

The masters are good with *dialogue.* Not just making it sound natural, but using it to advance a plot point or even to describe a character. It's actually part of the "show, don't tell" idea, a way to do so without slowing things down. Dialogue seems to flow more quickly than narrative. Susanna Kaysen makes use of dialogue-as-description extraordinarily well in *Girl, Interrupted.* At one point, she replicates a "representative" conversation between herself, as a patient in a psychiatric hospital, and a doctor. Notice how much this piece of dialogue tells us about her and about the doctor, without her having to use descriptive narrative:

> "Good morning. It has been decided that you were compulsively promiscuous. Would you like to tell me about that?"
>
> "No." This is the best of several bad responses, I've decided.
>
> "For instance, the attachment to your high school English teacher." Dr. Wick always uses words like *attachment.*

"Uh?"

"Would you like to tell me about that?"

"Um. Well. He drove me to New York." That was when I realized he was interested. He brought along a wonderful vegetarian lunch for me. "But that wasn't when it was."

"What? When what was?"

"When we f----d."

(Flush.) "Go on."

"We went to the Frick. I'd never been there. There was this Vermeer, see, this amazing painting of a girl having a music lesson—I just couldn't believe how amazing it was—"

"So when did you—ah—when was it?"

Doesn't he want to hear about the Vermeer? That's what I remember. "What?"

Think of all that can be inferred from just this short snippet of Kaysen's dialogue: the innocence and confusion of Kaysen and yet the depth and sensitivity; the discomfort, perhaps even inadequacy, of the doctor. All without being told these things. Dialogue is priceless, and the masters know how to use it.

Another key characteristic you'll notice from the masters is *flow*. The sentences just roll along—easily, effortlessly. Nothing is forced, nothing is choppy, nothing feels out of place. This becomes apparent if you read the stories out loud. Try it. Then try reading your own writing out loud. Strive for the flow of the masters. The words should just roll off your tongue. "If it sounds like writing," Elmore Leonard once said, "I rewrite it."

This gets back to the "ear" for writing idea I mentioned in the introduction—Mr. Reichenfeld's test. You have it or you don't.

But even if you have it, you should try to more fully develop it. There's another set of masters that can help you with that: the poets. This may seem like strange advice for people who want to write memoirs, but I would recommend that, besides reading great memoirs, you read yourself some great poetry. Poetry can sharpen not just your ear for flow but for *word choice*. Poetry is exacting. Poetry is all about using the perfect set of words to convey the meaning or mood you're trying to convey. You can read poetry from any era, but try to stick to the more contemporary poets who speak in today's language. Steer clear of the experimental, abstract stuff. Try some Billy Collins or Mary Oliver or Franz Wright or Mark Strand or Charles Simic. Mary Karr is a twofer, doubling as a memoirist *and* a poet. And then, try writing some poetry. Don't worry, you never have to show it to anybody, but writing poetry is an extraordinarily valuable exercise in how to choose the precise way of saying something (and a worthwhile endeavor in its own right). Learn when to write weep instead of cry, snicker instead of laugh, muck instead of dirt, scuttle instead of run.

Learn what you can from the masters. You'll be surprised by how much your writing will improve just by reading them. Great writing is contagious. But here's the thing about the masters: you're not them and you never will be. You'll never be Kaysen or Hemingway or Strayed or Nabakov. But that's okay! You can be you, with your own style and your own voice and your own story. When I used to read certain passages from the books above, I'd find myself wondering why I wrote at all. Mary Karr has written sentences I know I'm incapable of writing. In a million years I would never have described escalators the way she did. That kind of prose can be intimidating and more than a little discouraging. But over time, I've come to realize that comparing myself with other writers is a dead end. If you never win the Pulitzer Prize for literature, that doesn't mean you'll be wasting your time. You can still write an outstanding book. Or books! In fact, Hemingway himself seemed to understand that even the greats have their limits: "We all are apprentices in a craft where no one ever becomes a master." So maybe even the masters aren't masters.

Learn all you can from the great writers, hone your craft, and be who you are. Maybe you're not one of the greats, but you're a writer all the same.

CHAPTER FOUR

The Story of Your Life

*"All the world's a stage, and all the men
and women merely players."*

—WILLIAM SHAKESPEARE

Earlier we talked about memoir as story, and somewhere along the line, in some English or literary theory class, we've probably all learned about the narrative arc—a story's dramatic structure. And yet, the idea of a narrative arc seems to be an afterthought for most beginner memoirists. Why? Simple. People typically don't view their lives as *stories*. We go about our lives living one day at a time, and soon enough weeks go by and then months and then years. We don't ever seem to stop very long to examine where we've been or how we got to where we are. We don't see, in other words, the narrative arcs of our own lives. But they're there nevertheless, every bit as much as the narrative arcs of any story ever written.

As our lives progress, what happens to us seems random. We go here or we go there. We meet this person and then that person. We think we're in control and then some event pops up that changes things, maybe only slightly, maybe significantly. Then come other events, popping up here and there. Obstacles that we have to find ways to get around present themselves. Coincidences seem to jump into the picture occasionally, some meaningful, some not. We try to act, but it seems like most of the time we're only *re*acting to what is happening around us. We make plans, the plans go off without a hitch, we make other plans, and everything goes awry. Either way, we somehow keep going. And the days go by. Half the time we don't even notice what's happening to us, because it all unfolds so slowly, so gradually. How the heck did we get here? We don't really know because we don't spend time thinking about it. We're too busy living it, trying to get from one day to the next. From within, all the events of our lives just seem to sort of run together in a jumble and everything seems haphazard. The *last* thing it seems like is a coherent story!

Yet, a funny thing happens if you stop for a moment and look backward over your life. Really look over it. It looks a lot different than it looked as you lived it. When you take the time to examine it, to consider how you made it to this point in time, to step back and view it all objectively, darned if it doesn't look like, well, a *story*. And a carefully crafted one at that! Those random events that changed things suddenly seem less like random events and more like plot points. And the random people who have come in and out of your life start to resemble characters, some major, some just walk-on. In fact, very little seems random or coincidental. Even the coincidences start to reflect meaning. Everything suddenly seems to possess purpose. It's no longer a case of something happened and then something else happened. It's a case of something happened *because* something else happened. Everything becomes connected.

Face it. You're living a story. And if you're writing your memoirs, you need to start thinking that way. You're the main character in a fascinating play. Can you see it? It has drama, it has humor, it has pathos, tragedy, suspense, romance—why, there's something in there for the whole family. As said before, when you're writing your memoir, you need to convey more than just a dry recitation of facts and dates. Not just because you want to make a more compelling book, but because your *life* is not just a dry recitation of facts and dates. It's much, much more than that, and if you reduce it just to that, then you're missing the dramatic story that it really is.

A narrative arc can take different forms. Aristotle identified three major parts to a story: the beginning, providing background information, including introducing the characters; the middle, presenting us with a crisis in need of a solution; and the end, typically giving us the climax and the resolution to the crisis. Hence, we have the three-act play. In the nineteenth century, German playwright and novelist Gustav Freytag expanded on this idea a bit with what's now referred to as Freytag's pyramid, summarizing a story's structure as essentially a five-part deal.

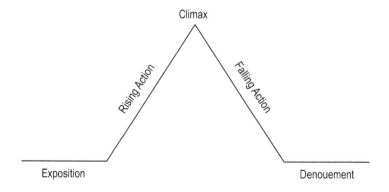

Exposition is the background information that leads to rising action (the crisis), ultimately leading to the dramatic climax. Then there's falling action as we catch our breath and the story begins to wind its way to a conclusion, and then the resolution—or dénouement if you want to impress your friends—where all the details get sown up nice and neatly. There's overlap, as you might guess, where some of the falling action bleeds into the resolution, and it's hard to tell the two apart. Every now and again you come across very dull arguments about how a resolution is subtly different than a dénouement, and some people even break it apart more by adding the term "conclusion" to the end so that you have falling action bleeding into resolution, then dénouement, then the conclusion. Outside tedious theory, it all pretty much runs together and it's more important to understand the basic structure than the details.

The point is, compelling stories have narrative arcs. Drama is built. Action rises and falls. If you're going to tell a compelling story, you'll find that it's fairly impossible to escape some form of this structure. A climax doesn't work very well without some buildup (rising action). The buildup loses steam if we don't know who the characters are, hence the need for exposition. We don't typically like to be left hanging, especially with true stories, and so a resolution is necessary.

For most memoirs, I'd like to offer this variation on the narrative arc, arrived at after years of cobbling memoirs together:

Turning Point → Exposition → Turning point revisited (climax?) → Recovery (and obstacles: another climax?) → Resolution/ transformation (message?)

When you're writing a memoir, it's tempting to start with exposition, isn't it? Collecting all the background material.

That's the beginning after all, right? Well, yes, but how do you know what background material you'll need if you haven't given thought to the true heart of the story? And the true heart of most memoirs lies in what I call the turning point. In literary theory, particularly with respect to fiction, you might hear this described as the "inciting event" or "catalyst." Every life has at least one of these moments. A life-altering moment. Something that helps define a person or at least heavily influences her. Or, if nothing else, something that just gets her life off track. Or on track, as the case may be.

It may not be readily apparent at first, but think about where you are now and what moment (or even series of moments) started you on your way there. It needn't be a hugely dramatic moment by the way. Typically, it's a moment of crisis that requires a resolution of some description, a hurdle that you had to clear to move forward with your life. Maybe it's somebody you met along the way who profoundly influenced you (for good or for bad). Or maybe it was just a key decision you had to make about your life. *This* is what you build your story around. This is where you start.

Here are some examples from clients I have worked with:

1   A man loses his infant son in an accident.

2   A woman, struggling all of her adult life with dissociative identity disorder, suddenly has a powerful flashback to a terrible childhood incident long since suppressed.

3   A woman who has made up her mind to commit suicide is prevented from doing so by an extraordinary set of circumstances.

4   At the age of thirteen, a Middle-Eastern girl is faced with the eventual prospect of an arranged marriage to someone she won't even know.

5   The leader of a criminal organization is arrested and convicted of drug trafficking.

I advise starting memoirs with the turning point. Done properly, the turning point becomes a hook to engage the reader. It needn't be long—just a few pages, maybe even a prologue, that describes this point in enough detail to interest the reader but leaves enough out to make him or her want to read on. Make the reader say, "Wow! What led to *that* moment in this person's life, and what happened next?" Get the reader to want to start turning the pages.

Then drop back to the exposition. Fill in the details on who you are and what took you to that momentous point. This is the backstory. It can be a chapter or a bunch of chapters. In the first example above, with the man losing his infant son, the turning point came relatively early in his life. He was only in his mid-twenties. Consequently, the exposition was relatively short. Most of the story took place after the turning point. That's fairly typical in a memoir. But in the second example, the woman struggling with dissociative identity disorder reached her turning point rather late in life. The exposition was rather long, as the reader learns about the gradual onset of her mental illness, her crying out for help, her problems with the psychiatric profession, repeated misdiagnoses, the lack of understanding from her husband and children, etc. Finally, a breakthrough moment occurs, which becomes the real turning point for her.

The exposition, then, leads us inexorably back to the turning point, and here the turning point can act as a kind of climax. The exposition can double as Herr Freytag's rising action, leading us to this climactic moment (and therefore providing the "arc" shape that my straight line above might appear to be missing), but a lot depends on the circumstances. There wasn't much that led to the death of the infant son, for instance. It was a sudden accident with no drama beforehand. But there was a long and winding road that led to the breakthrough moment for the woman with dissociative identity disorder. That breakthrough moment was a true climax in the way you might expect a climax in a Hollywood movie. In fact, the balance of the book was relatively short.

After the turning point—the moment of crisis, the life-altering event—we have what I refer to as the recovery. This is what you did about the event, or how it changed you, or how you got back on track, or how you just plain lived with it. The turning point is typically an obstacle (although not necessarily; it can sometimes be that breakthrough moment above), but the recovery generally contains its own obstacles, too. You know what you need to do, or want to do, but the doing is not without its problems. It can actually present us with more rising action pointing toward another climax. Will the main character recover? Will he or she clear these many hurdles? If so, how? In many memoirs, this is really the guts of the book. You want, or need, to get from Point A, where the turning point happened, to Point B, where everything is going to be okay again. Often, that journey is the true story.

The thing is, starting out, you may not even know what Point B looks like or that it even exists. And therein lies much of the tale. How did you get there? What did you have to do? Or how did you have to change? These are the questions alluded to earlier where your self-awareness is going to be required.

Let's revisit the examples above to see how the main characters "recovered" from the turning points in their respective lives.

1   A man loses his infant son in an accident. *From that point on, his life is never the same, and yet the memory of his son somehow motivates him and leads to a more courageous, more full life.*

2   A woman, struggling all of her adult life with dissociative identity disorder, suddenly has a powerful flashback to a terrible childhood incident long since suppressed. *The revelation leads her, finally, to mental well-being and peace of mind.*

3   A woman who has made up her mind to commit suicide is prevented from doing so by an extraordinary set of circumstances. *This initiates a complete reassessment of her life.*

4   At the age of thirteen, a Middle-Eastern girl is faced with the eventual prospect of an arranged marriage to someone she won't even know. *Seeking to escape her fate and, indeed, the very culture in which she is being raised, she spends her teen years considering where in the world to go and how to get there, ultimately moving to the United States, where she discovers freedom and happiness.*

5   The leader of a criminal organization is arrested and convicted of drug trafficking. *Time spent in prison wholly changes him.*

Of course these are but the most basic of summations. As mentioned, recoveries are not without their obstacles. The woman who reassessed her life after considering suicide actually endured tremendous struggle to find peace of mind, but the turning point at least gave her the motivation to keep going until, at last, she found it. The Middle-Eastern girl had a new set of problems to overcome once she made it to America. In fact, in her case, there was actually a second turning point and another recovery. More rising action and another climax.

In all of these cases, as with all good memoirs, going through the recoveries in some way *transformed* the characters. And there you have your *resolutions*. Think of resolutions as transformations. Somebody is a certain way, something happens to send them off course, and then (recovery) they're a different way. She's suicidal, and then she's life-embracing. She's trapped in a repressive culture, and then she's free. He's a hardened criminal, and then he's a gentle, law-abiding citizen. In all of these cases, the characters materially changed not just their circumstances, but, in a very real way, who they were.

Now, it must be said that the above examples are all rather dramatic. Most people don't experience such life-altering moments. They're not criminals, they've never struggled with mental illness, etc. But that doesn't mean their stories aren't interesting. They can be every bit as interesting, because the climactic moments that make up our lives, the dramatic turning points, no matter how small, speak to the human condition and the human condition is always interesting. If some point in life changed you in some way, then that point is dramatic, period. Find your turning point or points. Think about how you were ultimately transformed by them. Consider how different you are now from how you were then, and contemplate why that is. Fill in the exposition material and you've got yourself a narrative arc. *Voilà.* There's your story, the story of your life.

CHAPTER FIVE

Theme: Your Connection to the Reader

"A book is simply the container of an idea—like a bottle."

—ANGELA CARTER

In the last chapter we discussed the turning point. In truth, although there may be only one major turning point to a life, most lives have more than one, maybe even several. And in the recovery parts of their lives, most people may come across multiple obstacles, too. Many different hurdles they need to clear to get from Point A to Point B. If you're writing *a* memoir, you may just want to pick the most transforming moment to build your story around. If you're writing your memoir*s*, you'll be structuring several stories, each one perhaps independent of the rest. But if you want to produce a compelling book from front to back, all of them need to be somehow connected. And how does one connect a series of stories? Simple: by *theme*.

The theme of your work is what it's about—what it's *really* about. It's not just the story; it's what the story means. Whether you're focusing on one turning point in your life or fifty, overcoming one obstacle or a hundred, the theme is what ties the whole book together. It's the thread from which everything hangs. Without a cohesive theme, the book collapses into a pile of disconnected parts.

The story of the Middle-Eastern woman is a good example. Once she came to the United States, she had trouble assimilating to the new culture, making mistakes in love and marriage that created other crises. Overcoming her prospective destiny to be part of an arranged marriage to a stranger was only the first half of the book; the second half was her overcoming the difficulties of adjusting to her new country. In her case, the theme was her commitment and resolve toward making a life for herself that she deemed worthwhile. In both parts of the book, she overcame obstacles with courage and perseverance. The two halves of the book weren't separate stories, really. The book was the story of a woman who overcame, and the halves of the book were both exemplifications of this. One story (one theme), two expressions of it. If she'd had a different theme for the second half of the book—if, let's say, she became involved in drug trafficking after moving to the U.S. and was sent to prison where her experiences there changed her into a law-abiding citizen, if suddenly the theme wasn't overcoming cultural obstacles but instead atonement and redemption—I'd have recommended two separate books. The halves wouldn't have connected. There'd be no continuity. In a very real sense, it would have been two different books even if we'd have put them together between the same set of covers.

So what's the one major overall theme of your book? Of your life? That's what you have to uncover. It's there, believe me. If you don't know it, find it. Here's an exercise I recommend for all of my clients: think ahead to the future. Your book is printed. As a matter of fact, you're looking at a copy of it and it looks beautiful. Even though you were worried about the cover design, it came out perfect. You flip the book over and glance at the back cover, where, at the bottom, there's a picture of you (a very good picture!) and a brief paragraph providing the reader some biographical details. Above the picture, taking up the top half of the back cover, are about a hundred or so words briefly describing *what the book is about*.

What does it say there?

Take some time, in other words, to write your book description *before you even start writing your book*. And remember: the purpose of a cover book description is to sell the book, so make it compelling. "This is a book about George's life" isn't going to cut it. George needs to tell us why it's worth our time to read his book. George needs to engender some human interest. George needs to write something like this:

In 1969, at the age of nineteen, George McHugh, an introverted high-school dropout who's never ventured beyond the limits of his small Texas town, is drafted by the U.S. Army and sent half a world away to fight in the jungles of Vietnam. The lessons he learns there—about courage, about camaraderie, about leadership—will serve him well upon his return to the States. McHugh, with zero business experience but a newfound confidence and a rare appreciation for life earned by witnessing the

41

horrors of war, will go on to build the largest chain of supermarkets in the Southwest.

Can you see the theme? This is a book (not a real one, by the way) about business success and how it was attained by lessons learned as a soldier. It's about "courage and camaraderie and leadership" and about how George didn't possess any of these qualities at the start of his life but picked them up in the army.

The book is not about George, per se. It's about much more than George. This is often a difficult concept for beginning memoirists to grasp. As strange as it sounds, your memoir isn't about *you*. Not really. It's about something that links you to the human condition. It's that link—the theme!—that resonates with the reader. The theme connects more than just the many incidents included in the book. The theme connects you to the reader somewhere beyond both of you, in that shared space where we all experience the timeless truths of what it means to be human.

Write your book's description as an attempt to connect with the potential reader in that shared space. Write a description that answers the question, "Why should I care about your story?" and see how the theme presents itself. Then print that description out in bold font and keep it on your desk, right beside your computer keyboard. As you write your book, you'll want to keep glancing at it to make certain that you're tying your story together around that theme and heading toward an eventual resolution that properly reflects it.

Note what the theme is not: it's not what you did or where you went or even what you experienced. The theme of George's book isn't that he went to Vietnam and witnessed the atrocities of war and then came home and ultimately became a business success. Sure, that's what the book is about, but only on the surface. That's not what it's really about deep down. Going to war, coming home, becoming a business success—none of this is theme. It's plot. Done properly, it will reflect the theme, but the difference is the proverbial difference between the trees and the forest.

Unless it's autobiography, where you're getting all the details down for posterity, trim the pieces of your life that don't connect to your theme. If, in getting from Point A to Point B, something major or even entertaining happened that nevertheless doesn't really help lead to your story's resolution, then think twice about including it. Memoirs that are poorly constructed often have a bunch of these. They're called digressions, and, at best, they make the story seem meandering and unfocused. At worst, they act like red herrings; we expect that somehow the digression will tie in with the rest of the story. When it doesn't, we're left perplexed. That week you spent in Rome, although a terrific memory that might make for a good short story on its own, probably doesn't need to be included in the memoir you're writing about how you rose to prominence in the Indiana state senate. Now, if the story of Rome somehow helps the reader understand you better—if something happened that effectively illustrates some character trait of yours that had a bearing on your political career—then leave it in. But if it doesn't connect with the theme in some way, think long and hard about including it.

Here's the thing about the theme, and the same could be said about the whole narrative arc of your story: it might very well change the further into the book you get. Remember the discussion in Chapter One about learning about yourself by writing? Here's where this becomes apparent. Until you really examine your life in the way that only writing about it can make possible, you may not even see the turning points, or the obstacles or their effects. It might not be until chapter twelve that you see that a minor incident you devoted a short paragraph to in chapter three was, in reality, a major event that changed your life. You may not see how you were affected, how you were transformed. You may start out your memoir on hiking across Europe with a general theme about perseverance but then end up with a theme about the universality of compassion once you realize—by writing about them—how so many people you met along the way went out of their way to help you. The book you end up with may be a different book than the one you started with. It's amazing (and fascinating) how many times this happens.

Understand the narrative arc and understand the importance of tying things to a theme. And start writing. But don't carve anything in stone. Keep an open mind, knowing that your arc and your theme are tentative. Chances are good that they're not going to change. But they may, and that's okay. In fact, if it leads to one of those *aha!* moments, it's much better than okay.

Still, you have to start somewhere. So, with at least an idea of what the theme is that you're going to build your memoir around, and an idea of your story's narrative arc, let's move ahead to getting this rocket off the ground.

CHAPTER SIX

Building Your Birdhouse

"Outlining is like putting on training wheels. It gives me the courage to write, but we always go off the outline."

—HALLIE EPHRON

I have a small woodshop at my house. Last spring I started building a birdhouse. It seemed a simple enough task. So simple, in fact, that I didn't even bother with any plans. Not so much as a sketch. I had it all in my head and I just jumped in, cutting the wood and slapping it all together, figuring I'd have it done in a couple of days. And when it was finished? I don't know; I never finished it. Not surprisingly, nothing fit quite right and time and time again I came upon little problems I had not foreseen. The pieces are still sitting on my workbench. Lately, I've been thinking of using them to make a hat rack.

I know a lot of people who could tell a similar tale about writing their memoirs. Nothing fits quite right and unforeseen problems develop. And ultimately the pieces sit undisturbed on the desk as a stack of pages or in a desktop folder that never gets clicked opened anymore. Just a reminder that we could all benefit from spending some quality time in the planning stages.

No matter how well you think you know your story, draw yourself a plan. That is to say, write up an *outline*. Don't worry about making it fancy like you learned in school with Roman numerals followed underneath by capital letters with Arabic numbers underneath those, followed by lower-case letters and then lower-case Roman numerals. Who has that kind of patience (or time)? Your teacher isn't going to see this. This is just for you. You don't even have to use numbers or letters. Scribble it out like you would a grocery list. Write it on a cocktail napkin. Just get something down.

Hopefully, by the time you write your outline, you've given enough thought to the project to where you have a good idea of what your narrative arc looks like. So, maybe the first item on your list is your turning point. Then the next items will comprise the exposition part of your arc, the part that took you there. Make a list of the background items your reader will need to know, information about you and the other characters, places, and events—all the things that will eventually land you back at the turning point. Then make a list of the items that comprise the recovery. Again, people, places, and events. It helps to place them chronologically but, to start, just get everything down on paper. Brainstorm. Get yourself into stream-of-consciousness mode and just regurgitate everything you think belongs. At the start, don't leave anything out; you can always cut stuff out later.

Then start putting everything into an order. Your list—your rudimentary outline—might look something like this:

BUILDING YOUR BIRDHOUSE

Turning Point: Bankruptcy. Millionaire to failure.
Exposition:
Growing up in Brooklyn. Description of
   neighborhood.

Values learned from Mom, including that story
   about what happened when I got caught
   cheating on the spelling test in 3rd grade.
Noticing kids in school with money, esp. Joey
   Rubis, the rich kid whose dad gave him a
   convertible.
Going to work in Uncle's Rico's pizza shop.
Going to work for contractor and learning the
   trade.
Saving money and learning value of hard work,
   including the story of me being able to buy
   my first set of wheels.
Flipping houses, story of the very first one!
Making lots of money.
Expanding way too fast.
Living FAR beyond my means! Include the story
   about buying the Maserati.
Piling up debt. That time my credit card was first
   rejected (on a dinner date!)

Bankruptcy (Turning Point revisited)
Humiliation.
Mom's disappointment. Her silence when I told her.

Recovery
Uncle's motivational talk to me.
Going back to work.

My new "one-person" contracting business. Story
   here about that first rehab project.
Initial struggles. Wondering if I can make it.
Gradual regaining of trust from vendors. Put in
   the story of Brad from the hardware store,
   saying he believed in me.
Money finally coming in, corner has been turned!
Gradual accumulation of a million dollars' net
   worth again. Back on top!
Lessons from bankruptcy: anecdote about buying
   a Kia instead of a Maserati!

Ending? Something about Mom here?

Okay, as far as outlines go, this is a great start. Lots of key points. Now, upon closer examination, it should become apparent that certain items on the list seem to belong together, either chronologically or conceptually. Once it's all down on paper, you might look at your list and decide to clump some of the items together, dividing the list like this:

Turning Point: Bankruptcy. Millionaire to failure.
Exposition:
Growing up in Brooklyn. Description of
   neighborhood.
Values learned from Mom, including that story
   about what happened when I got caught
   cheating on the spelling test in 3rd grade.
Noticing kids in school with money, esp. Joey
   Rubis, the rich kid whose dad gave him a
   convertible.

Going to work in Uncle's Rico's pizza shop.

Going to work for contractor and learning the trade.

Saving money and learning value of hard work,
    including the story of me being able to buy
    my first set of wheels.

Flipping houses, story of the very first one!

Making lots of money.

Expanding way too fast.

Living FAR beyond my means! Include the story
    about buying the Maserati.

Piling up debt. That time my credit card was
    first rejected (on a dinner date!)

Bankruptcy (Turning Point revisited)

Humiliation.

Mom's disappointment. Her silence when I told her.

Recovery

Uncle's motivational talk to me.

Going back to work.

My new "one-person" contracting business. Story
    here about that first rehab project.

Initial struggles. Wondering if I can make it.

Gradual regaining of trust from vendors. Put in
    the story of Brad from the hardware store,
    saying he believed in me.

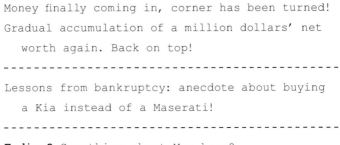

Now, there's no right or wrong to this, but if I were writing this outline, I would split up the list as above. I would anticipate that in the book, there would be a section on growing up that would include values learned from Mom and experiences at school. There would be another section on early work experiences, perhaps one part dedicated just to the first real success. And so forth. I'm sure you can see what's happening here: we're creating ideas for *chapters*. I count eleven of them if we're including the prologue. We've now got our chapter list, a tentative table of contents. The book is already taking shape!

And you have something even more important. What you have now is your plan. This is your instruction sheet, the thing I was without when I started my birdhouse, the thing a lot of memoirists are without before they start typing out their story.

But it gets even better. You know what you really have? You have a monumental undertaking that, although at first glance seemed completely overwhelming (the writing of your memoir!), now is broken down into manageable, achievable pieces. Believe me, this becomes very reassuring. You eat an elephant one bite at a time, goes the old saying, and so from this point on, you don't have to worry about eating the entire elephant. In other words, you don't have to write an entire book. You only have to worry about writing a chapter of a book. That becomes your ongoing task. And then the next chapter, and then the next.

When I write a book, I like to take the outline and coordinate it with a calendar. Much depends on your schedule and how much time you can devote to your memoir in any given week. I like to shoot for a first draft in about six months, approximately 180 days. If I was writing the above memoir, that would mean sixteen days per chapter, or about two weeks. That would be my goal then: one chapter every two weeks. That would become my focus, and I'd do everything I could to meet that goal. Only you know what motivates you to finish a job. For me, I have to have deadlines. If a project doesn't have a due date, I'm much more likely to drop it down on my list of priorities.

Now, here's the difference between an outline for a memoir and plans for a birdhouse: the outline will change. Most certainly in fact. Realize that your outline can only ever be a tentative one. Sure enough, by the time you get to chapter two or three, you're going to have to revisit the balance of the outline. You're going to remember something you forgot to put in. You're going to recognize that something early in the book had much more of a profound effect on your life than you thought when you wrote the outline, meaning that some earlier chapter might need to be added, or perhaps some other chapter ought to be deleted. Maybe one chapter becomes so full and so long that it needs to be broken into two chapters, or more. Or maybe late in the book, you find yourself writing about some incident that makes you realize more expository detail is needed early in the book, maybe a whole new chapter. Maybe, as we talked about in Chapter Five, you discover another turning point. Maybe your whole narrative arc gets thrown off.

Don't be discouraged. All of this defines a little concept that I like to call the *creative process*. And it's positively beautiful. It might not look pretty as it's happening; it might be exceedingly frustrating, in fact, but the result can be amazing, like the proverbial pearl that comes about as a result of irritation. Just go with it, is my advice. I have noticed in almost every memoir I've written that somewhere along the line, typically somewhere past the tentative halfway point, the outline becomes (at least somewhat) obsolete and the book itself tells you which way to go. At this point, you're no longer writing the book; the book is writing itself and you're more or less along for the ride. This is the way it is with art, and memoir is nothing less than art. It's Michelangelo's idea of chipping away at a stone to reveal the sculpture that's within, just waiting to be made manifest. Your story is there, someplace, and little by little it begins to reveal itself without a lot of additional planning and organizing. You just have to pay attention to the clues. Chapter six lets you know what chapter seven should be. It might be nothing like the original chapter seven from your outline, but that's because when you wrote the outline, you really had only the roughest idea in your head as to what chapters one through six would look like.

All that said, you still need an outline to begin. The outline forces you to think through the book, to nail down the real story and to visualize its structure. Writing it out may even cause you to rethink what you thought the theme or arc would be. It also gives you a means by which to get started, maybe the hardest part of all. It's the first tangible step on the journey. Theme and narrative arc are more abstract and less quantifiable. When you're writing the outline, you're finally putting words to page. You're starting to write.

CHAPTER SEVEN

Writing. Reading. Rewriting.

"I'm doin' the work! I'm baby-steppin'! I'm not a slacker!"

—BILL MURRAY IN *What About Bob*

With the outline, as discussed in the last chapter, you can break your book-writing project into manageable pieces. From here on, it's just chapter by chapter. So, write chapter one. From your outline, you should have a solid idea of what chapter one should contain. But you may not have thought through all the details just yet. The time to do that is before you start writing it. What you'll need is another outline—a sort of mini-outline that encompasses just this chapter's material.

The mini-outline is created more or less the same way as the main outline: brainstorm for ideas. Think about all the people and events and places that need to be touched on in chapter one and put them all down. Think in terms of the five W's from the field of journalism: who, what, where, when, and why.

Remember, as we talked about earlier, to think especially in terms of "why." And remember to ask "how." Consider everything in terms of motivations and effects.

Write it all down (again informally), and then sort it all into a workable order (probably chronologically). And then off you go, ready, finally, to start the process of writing your memoir.

It is at this precise moment that some people get stuck. The planning, the outlining, the thinking about it—all the preliminary stuff is out of the way, and now it comes down to actually forming complete sentences. Actual prose! It can be intimidating. This is what the whole world is going to someday read! Your kids, your co-workers, your ninth grade English teacher who never gave you anything higher than a "C" on anything you ever wrote for her. Everybody! Don't be surprised if, right around this time, you go to sleep one night and have one of those dreams where you're standing naked at the front of a classroom.

What many people do at this point is go back to the outline. "Let's just make sure I have everything right," they'll say to themselves. "No sense in being hasty." And they'll rewrite the outline, examine it, rewrite it again, tweak it, add to it, delete from it—all the while convincing themselves that what they're doing is writing. They're not. They're still planning. In fact, what they're really doing is stalling.

I remember a sales job I had right out of college. It entailed cold calling a list of potential business prospects. We salespeople were educated on the product and trained on how to sell it. We spent several days practicing our cold calls, doing role-playing with each other. Then the day came to actually start calling real people. I was given a stack of three-by-five index cards of prospective customers from the sales manager and wished "good luck!" All ready to go, I sat in my cubicle, picked up the phone, and...put it back down again. Maybe, I thought, it would help if I read the information on the cards first to acquaint myself with who these people are. Make sure I can pronounce their names, for instance. And maybe there's a better order in which to call them. The stack is in alphabetical order, but maybe I should categorize the prospects geographically. Maybe what I ought to do is practice the call one more time, do a little more role-playing. Or even better, educate myself more on the product, just to make certain I can answer any question put to me. Before long, the whole morning went by and I hadn't made a single call. But if somebody were to have asked me what I was doing that morning, I would have told them I was cold calling. I was selling. But I was doing neither. (As it happened, somebody *did* ask: the sales manager. After a brief, rather one-sided consultation, we came to the mutual understanding that I would actually make some real calls or seek employment elsewhere.)

Don't stall. Take a deep breath and remember that what you first write down is most likely *not* what the whole world is going to someday read. Your English teacher isn't going to see it. There's going to be plenty of time later for rewriting and polishing. The key at this point is to just get the material down. Throw it down on the page as best you can. Write a sentence, read it, improve upon it if you can, and then write the next sentence. Baby steps. One in front of the other. And just keep going.

Ultimately, you're going to baby-step your way through chapter one. Congratulate yourself and then re-read the chapter, rewriting it as you see fit. Make sure it's good, but don't worry about making it great. Not yet. The time for that will come later, after the first draft of the entire book is done. Remember, the creative process will necessarily mean that changes to your book are coming. Even if you could make chapter one "perfect," it's not going to remain perfect for long. Something will come along later that will force you to revisit it: a character you need to introduce, an incident that happened that you need to provide more detail about. Whatever change is in store, you're probably not going to see it until you get further into the book, so don't worry about it now. Just move on to chapter two and repeat the process you used for chapter one, including more brainstorming and another mini-outline.

This idea of just getting the material down is no excuse for laziness, by the way. Even though it's just a first draft, it should go without saying that as you're writing it, you'll want to write it as best you can. The point is to set aside the inherent perfectionism that plagues the typical writer. Maybe it's insecurity, but we writers think we can always improve upon our work. The thing is, we're probably right about that. There's almost always a better way to say something. Walt Whitman used to revise his poems even after they were published. This, however, is not the time for that level of scrutiny. But setting aside the perfectionism isn't license for sloppiness, either. You'll have plenty of work to do when you ultimately go back and do the rewrites and revisions of your whole manuscript and there's no sense in making extra work for yourself then by being careless now. Write something you can feel good about. Write it, read it, rewrite it if necessary, but then move on.

Repeat the process for chapter two and then three and then four and then five and then—eventually—chapter by chapter, you're going to find yourself in possession of the first draft of your memoir. Congratulate yourself again. But then get ready.

There's a *lot* of work ahead. At this point, you'll want to find a quiet place somewhere to read the whole manuscript from front to back. Go ahead and make minor tweaks as you go along. Restructure a sentence that you observe needs help, replace a word here or there with a better one, correct spelling and punctuation errors.

Mostly, however, take notes. There are two major questions you need to be asking yourself as you read, and several less major ones (I hesitate to use the word "minor" because they're pretty important, too, as we'll see).

The major questions:

- Is my story true to its theme?
- Have I followed my narrative arc?

The (honest) answers to these questions will tell you a lot about your book and the initial job you've done. As we discussed in Chapter Six, the creative process may well have swept in and changed your arc. Or even your theme. That honest searching we talked about earlier in the book, the "how" and "why" questions that you should have been asking yourself as you were writing to better flesh out your motivations and your story, all of this might have produced a different book than the one you thought you were going to write. In the writing process, you've learned a lot about yourself, and that may well have changed some things. Maybe it's changed everything.

Naturally, these discoveries might produce some work. Perhaps a lot of work. But I find the kind of wholesale changes that self-discoveries produce in a memoir are typically limited to the first few chapters. Once the self-discoveries are revealed, the writing of the book more or less follows upon the course the self-discoveries dictate. You'll probably need more revisions earlier in the manuscript than later.

The real questions, in other words, are these: is the draft true to the (by now) better-defined theme? Does the draft follow the new, or revised, or more focused narrative arc? If these major components of the book have changed, does the entire draft reflect those changes? If not, highlight those places—segments, paragraphs, perhaps whole chapters—that are going to need to be revised. Make notes about the order of the book. Given what you know now, should the material in chapter seven be introduced earlier? Maybe in chapter three? Should certain characters be introduced in different ways or at different times?

Incidentally, don't feel like you've done something wrong, or incomplete, if your theme or narrative arc haven't so much as wavered. It might just be that you were extraordinarily self-aware before you even started the project. You knew right off the bat what the theme of your story was and nothing you discovered changed it. You might still have uncovered some things about yourself, but nothing so dramatic as to alter the overall structure of the manuscript. The book has taken you exactly to where you set out to go. And you've been honest, too. Good for you. That happens, and it's a testament to a life well examined and a book well thought out. But keep an open mind, just in case. It could be that, upon your reading of the manuscript, you notice parts of the story simply don't adhere to your narrative arc properly. Events are out of order, or maybe some events don't even belong. These kinds of departures from the original plan are pretty common. It's not the narrative arc that's changed (or the theme, for that matter); it's just that the information hasn't supported it properly in spots. Flag those spots.

Okay, with those major questions uppermost in your mind as you're reading, allowing you to make certain your book is structured appropriately and centered consistently on its given theme, you'll also want to keep in mind some less major questions that take us into the real guts of the writing—questions of description and style and flow. Let's examine those next.

CHAPTER EIGHT

Spotting the Weaknesses

*"I think I did pretty well, considering I started
out with nothing but a bunch of blank paper."*

—STEVE MARTIN

When the first draft of your manuscript is completed, you'll want
to read it with an eye toward making certain you've properly
incorporated the two big conceptual elements of your memoir—
theme and narrative arc. But you'll also want to make certain
you've properly handled some of the more modest (yet collectively just as important) elements. No doubt your manuscript has
some weaknesses (everybody's does), and you need to be able to
spot those weaknesses and fix them. As you're reading your draft,
make sure to ask yourself these questions:

• Are the important characters fully fleshed out?

- Are the pivotal moments described in adequate detail? Have I sufficiently shown, not told?

- Is there enough dialogue? Does it sound natural?

- Does the writing flow?

- Does each chapter transition well to the chapter that follows?

- Have I sufficiently built the drama?

- Are there any digressions that ought to be cut?

- Does the writing sound like *me*?

These are all critical, and so, in no particular order, let's look at all of them a little closer.

Having the important characters fully fleshed out and the pivotal moments described in adequate detail might not happen in the first draft, and there's usually an interesting reason for that: until the draft is completed, you sometimes don't know just who the important characters or what the pivotal moments are!

It's only in the re-reading that you're able to see that Aunt Gertie had the profound effect on your life that she did. And yet, you don't even describe her. Or how about that time you lost the election for class president in high school? It was a loss, so you glossed over it in your book. But in thinking about it—by reading what you wrote about it and seeing how it was connected to the events of your life that followed—you now realize that, even in defeat, the experience whetted your appetite for politics, your eventual life's work. Maybe the experience deserves more than the one measly paragraph you gave it. In the memoir I helped write for the drug kingpin, there was a rather long section on the federal investigation that led to his eventual arrest but only a couple short paragraphs on the friend who helped set him up. As interesting as the investigation was, the friend's betrayal was the really dramatic part. And yet, in reading our first draft, we could see the investigation had gotten most of our attention. The friend needed much more print than what we had given him. Get the idea? When you look back on your life—by reading about it!—you'll see which parts of your manuscript need to be more fully developed and which people need to be more fleshed out.

How to go about these tasks? Let's start with character description. It's more than just physical attributes, although it can certainly be those, too. "Scott was handsome, but in a boyish-looking, maybe even effeminate way" isn't a bad start. But let's see how Ernest Hemingway described F. Scott Fitzgerald in *A Moveable Feast:*

> Scott was a man then who looked like a boy with a face between handsome and pretty. He had very fair wavy hair, a high forehead, excited and friendly eyes and a delicate long-lipped Irish mouth that, on a girl, would have been the face of a beauty. His chin was well built and he had good ears and a handsome, almost beautiful, unmarked nose. This should not have added up to a pretty face, but that came from the coloring, the very fair hair and the mouth. The mouth worried you until you knew him and then it worried you more.

Hemingway gets into more than just physical characteristics here. He's building a portrait that may also say something about Fitzgerald's personality. (It might also say something about the main character—Hemingway himself.) Either way, Hemingway has given us an indelible description that will stay with us as we read on to learn more about the two men's interactions.

In other words, description is more than just height and weight and hair color. Give the readers a picture, something they can keep in their mind's eye. But give them some hints at the character's personality, too. Give them both. Sometimes a quirk helps. The way your brother arched his eyebrows or the way your best friend almost skipped when she walked. An accent. A word he or she always mispronounced. Those god-awful, oversized round glasses from 1986 that he was still wearing in 2002. The ever-present cigar. Her overuse of perfume. Just something a reader can glom on to as the book progresses so he or she can picture the character whenever the character makes an appearance. But round the character out, too. These are human beings we're talking about, and the word is "character," not "caricature." Of course your narrative should help with this. Important characters should come to life as the book progresses and we read about their actions. The actions should support the descriptions and vice versa.

As for pivotal moments, there are probably as many ways to describe these as there are moments. In general terms, you need to properly set the scene: time of day, inside or outside, maybe the weather, lighting, atmosphere, etc. Put the reader mentally into the scene. Don't go overboard with adjectives! A few well-placed, well-thought-out ones ought to suffice. See how Cheryl Strayed describes the heat in this scene in *Wild*:

As I hiked, I moaned again and again, as if that would provide some cooling relief, but nothing changed. The sun still stared ruthlessly down on me, not caring one iota whether I lived or died. The parched scrub and scraggly trees still stood indifferently resolute, as they always had and always would.

In about fifty words, Strayed sets a scene we can actually feel. The scrub is "parched." The trees are "scraggly." Notice how they become almost like characters, standing "indifferently resolute." Meanwhile, the sun didn't shine down; it "stared ruthlessly down." Strayed's not telling, she's showing. She could have just written: *It was hot that day.* But then we couldn't have mentally joined her on her hike. We wouldn't have become involved in the story.

Think about the senses and go beyond the obvious one, sight. How did something taste? Smell? Feel? Sound? Painting a picture for the reader can be done in more ways than just visually. Drop your reader into the scene by making sure he or she is getting a full impression.

Keep in mind we're referring at this point to pivotal scenes. Not every scene needs to be endlessly described. Some scenes are more important than others. Keep the book moving. Don't dawdle. The description needs to support the story. The passage above from Strayed's book is fairly early and it's critical in helping us get a feel for the challenges she would face during her trek of the Pacific Crest Trail. It had a purpose, in other words. Description just for the sake of description is filler begging to be cut.

Go easy on adverbs—the "ly" words—in your descriptions. Strayed uses "ruthlessly" and "indifferently," but both are necessary, it seems to me, given the context. But when I'm editing books, I frequently see far too many unnecessary ones. Examples that have crossed my desk:

- We lamentably mourned.
- The two sides agreeably compromised.
- She began to loudly shout.

See the problem? Is there a way to shout other than loudly? "The road to hell is paved with adverbs," said Stephen King. It's tempting to want to modify *everything* with a descriptive word. Resist the temptation.

Resist the temptation to use complex metaphors, too. Metaphors and similes can be effective, but they're most effective when they're simple. Strayed uses an implied metaphor with her description of the sun. She personifies it by describing it as ruthlessly staring at her. The sun becomes as a person. Simple. Effective. A lot of beginning writers feel the need to write something more involved, to somehow prove themselves as writers. In the hands of a lesser writer, this might have become something like: "The sun stared down at me like a judge from some hellish courtroom, moments before banging his gavel down and sentencing me to death by heat and thirst."

I think I like Strayed's better. The beginning writer is trying too hard, calling to mind those tortured metaphors and similes that get emailed around every so often. You might have read them. Here are a few of my favorites:

McBride fell twelve stories, hitting the pavement like a Hefty bag filled with vegetable soup.

John and Mary had never met. They were like two hummingbirds that had also never met.

The little boat gently drifted across the pond exactly the way a bowling ball wouldn't.

I'm sure you get the idea. If you re-read the metaphors and similes you've used in your manuscript and they seem as tortured as these, do the reader a favor and either simplify them or, better yet, cut them out altogether. Great metaphors are things of literary beauty. Bad ones are like, well, something really bad.

One way to make description especially effective (both for character and plot), and to show rather than tell, is through dialogue. Recall Susanna Kaysen's example in Chapter Three from *Girl, Interrupted*. Dialogue breathes life into a scene. You can either write: *John and I argued about it, with him asking something about why there's evil if God exists and me talking about the existence of human free will*, or you can create a dialogue out of this, which would probably be pretty interesting. Don't tell us what you both said. Let us hear it for ourselves. Bring us into the room and let us listen to the discussion.

But make it natural. Our contract with the reader allows us to fudge a bit if we don't remember precisely what was said word for word, but it still at least needs to *sound* real. People use contractions when they speak. "Let us go" should probably be written, "Let's go." People have a tendency to not use big words in their day-to-day conversations. He probably called you "cheap," not "parsimonious." You probably called him "lazy," not "indolent." And make sure the dialogue is consistent with the particular character who's speaking. Think like a method actor—get inside your character's head and think about the way he most likely said the line you gave him, knowing all that you know or remember about him. Finally, read your dialogue out loud and see if it sounds real.

Speaking of reading out loud, do this also to check your manuscript's flow. Does the prose flow smoothly? You don't have to read the whole manuscript out loud, but if you come across a part that seems forced, or awkward, or just plain too bogged down, see if it passes the ear test. If it doesn't, rewrite it until it does. Beware of choppiness. Too many short sentences in a row. This takes away from flow. It makes the reading jerky. It sounds like the sentences you're now reading. Maybe I should have written them like so: Beware of choppiness, which can be caused by too many short sentences in a row, interfering with the book's flow and making the reading sound jerky.

There's flow in the words, and there's flow in the structure. Does the narrative itself flow well? Does one passage lead naturally into the next? How are your segues—natural sounding or forced? Does each chapter transition well from the chapter before? Pay attention to how you end chapters. Nothing keeps a reader engaged like a powerful chapter ending that provides some kind of foreshadowing or dramatic turn of events. Think of the way good television dramas keep you from changing the channel during commercials by providing something sensational right before the commercial break. It's the same thing at the end of the episode, right before the line pops us that says, *To be continued...* And then the screen goes black. Think in terms of a good "blackout" line.

Here's one of my own:

> I understood what (the vision) meant. The basement was from our house in Lac-Mégantic. The body was mine. I was seven years old. My father had killed me, or at least he thought he had. And then he had buried me alive.[1]

---

[1] *Ellevie*, Marcelle Evie Guy, 2014 (Blue Fluke Media). With kind permission.

You don't need to know the context to understand that something important just happened, something in this person's understanding. Something that we want to know more about. There's more explanation ahead and, perhaps, some resolution. The reader wants to get there. *What's coming next?*

Sometimes a good blackout line just presents itself even if you're not ready to end the chapter. In the above case, my client and I still had material we wanted to put into this particular chapter. But the chapter was plenty long enough as it was, and when we hit upon this passage, it just seemed like the perfect place to instill a little drama by bringing the chapter to a close. The chapter just seemed to want to end with that paragraph. Listen to what your writing is saying to you. When a chapter wants to end, let it.

Building drama is all about presenting the reader with enough information to keep them interested, but not enough to give away the whole story. "Make them laugh, make them cry, but most of all, make them wait," said Charles Dickens. Blackout lines work because they provide hints that further information is coming without saying what the information is. But Dickens's principle holds throughout the book, not just at chapter endings. Always make sure you're leaving things for the reader to discover later. Hint at them. Make use of foreshadowing. Leave something—something big—for the resolution. Don't use chapter one to tell us how your life turned out and what you learned along the way. Leave the reader treasures to discover.

Look for needless digressions as you're reading your manuscript, too. We touched on this earlier in respect to the theme. Just as we can underestimate the importance of certain events or people, so can we overestimate. Ask yourself if the incident or character in question really adds anything to the plot. Could the story survive without it? But be careful. A minor incident is still capable of speaking volumes about you, your life, or another character. But if the incident adds nothing, if it doesn't better describe you (or your life or another character), if it doesn't, in other words, serve to *advance the story* in any appreciable way, then consider chopping it out. Your readers will thank you for keeping the story on track.

Finally, make sure the prose sounds like you. To be genuine, the memoir has to be in your voice. Personally, I happen to think people make more out of this than it warrants. Whole books have been written on voice and most books on memoir writing seem to devote at least a chapter to it. It's an easy thing to overthink and overanalyze. Look, just make sure you're not trying to be somebody else when you're writing. That's all. Don't use words you wouldn't normally use and don't keep asking yourself, "How would Mary Karr say this?"

But remember, too, that people don't necessarily write the way they talk. It's okay to use a thesaurus once in a while to come up with that perfect word for the context, even if you've never in your life spoken that word aloud. Just do it for the right reason. If there's a better word, more appropriate, more descriptive, use it. And it's okay to read a sentence from your manuscript and know, intuitively, that it can be improved upon based on great memoirs you've read. You don't have to imitate Mary Karr, but you can certainly allow her writing to inspire you to do better. Ultimately, the more you write, the more your particular "voice" will come through. Every writer has his or her own style and the style comes about organically over time. You won't be able to help it. You have a natural voice, and if you write enough, it will reveal itself. And that's all you need to know about voice.

Okay, you've read the manuscript and spotted the weaknesses. Maybe you've fixed the minor ones as you went along. Fine. Major ones should just be noted until you've finished reading the whole thing. Don't cut out an apparent digression in chapter three that, when you're reading chapter eleven, you suddenly realize was necessary for the book to make sense.

So now go back and strengthen the weaknesses. Rewrite, add, cut, or do whatever you need to do to improve your manuscript. Then, congratulate yourself yet one more time. You've worked hard and accomplished much. Now there's only one thing to do: go back through and do it all again.

CHAPTER NINE

Fumbling Towards Objectivity

*"I have rewritten—often several times—every word
I have ever published. My pencils outlast their erasers."*

—VLADIMIR NABOKOV, Speak, Memory

Your second time through your manuscript should be just as thorough as your first time. But it helps if it's something else as well: *objective*. In the romantic sci-fi drama *The Eternal Sunshine of the Spotless Mind*, people are able to go through a procedure where certain things can be erased from their memories. Everything else about their memories remains intact. I've often wished this kind of procedure was available for writers. If there's one major, inherent problem we all face, it's the lack of objectivity that comes about because we're just so blindly close to our work. How valuable would it be if, when we reach the end of the book we're writing, we could just have the memory of its writing erased from our brains? The only thing we'd remember is that we wrote *something*. That way we could sit down and read it as if for the first time. Imagine what we could spot with that kind of objectivity.

Alas, there is no such procedure, and friends in the scientific community tell me that none is forthcoming, at least anytime soon. (I'm going to remain hopeful nonetheless.) Meanwhile, here's the next best thing: *time*. Time can at least dull the memory. So take your manuscript, after you've made your first-time-through rewrites, and stick it in a drawer and don't look at it for a month. Or longer. Obviously, the longer the better, but try to hold out for at least thirty days. Try not to even think about it. Start writing something else in the meantime. Go on vacation. Get away from your book, in other words.

It won't be as though you'd never seen it before when you finally sit down with it again, but it won't look as familiar as it did. You'll see some issues with it that you hadn't noticed before, I guarantee you. Of course, this can be discouraging. You'll read a certain paragraph and hear yourself saying things like, "Who wrote *this*?!" and, "What in God's name was I thinking?!" Relax. It's perfectly natural. Happens all the time. In fact, if you don't react like this a few times, you probably need to stick the manuscript back in the drawer for a couple more weeks. Just be thankful you didn't try to get it published right after that first draft.

Go through your manuscript this second time asking yourself all the same questions we covered in the last two chapters. Then, after any additional edits and rewrites, it's time to get an even more objective view. Now is the time to let a trusted friend or family member read it, a "beta" or test reader. But make sure it's someone you can trust to be honest with you. You probably have people in your life that would beam and call you Shakespeare if you handed them an excerpt of a random page you copied out of the phone book. God bless these people. We need them. But not right now. What we need now is honesty, even brutal honesty. We need criticism.

We also need an intelligent opinion. If your cousin has always been brutally honest with you but has never read a book in his entire adult life, you might want to consider someone else. Who's the reader in your family or circle of friends, the one who's always carrying a book around? Get a hold of that person.

Intelligence and honesty. And time-sensitivity. Don't hand it to someone who's going to take a year with it. Can they commit to reading it in a reasonable period of time? Sixty days? Ninety?

Preferably, you should have two of these people. Even more preferable, they shouldn't know each other. They shouldn't be in positions where they can discuss your manuscript with each other, compare notes, and influence each other. You want two completely objective people considering your work separately. If two is better, then how about three? Three is probably too many. Trying to sift through an excess of opinions can lead to confusion and uncertainty, especially if those opinions significantly diverge. It's the too-many-chefs syndrome, the conundrum of the committee approach. Stick with two very trusted, very honest people.

Be open-minded to their suggestions and criticisms. Tell your ego to get lost. There's no room for defensiveness in your attempt to make your book as good as it can be. At this point, it's not about you; it's about your book. You've come this far and your obligation now is to serve your manuscript to the best of your ability, and that may well mean having to admit that your book—as good as you thought it was—could stand to be improved upon. In the end, however, trust your own instincts. If something your test readers suggest doesn't sit right with you, if to your mind it doesn't make your book *better*, then skip it. Be true to yourself and your unique vision for the book.

By the way, this is the perfect time to select the book's title. I know what you're thinking: this late in the game? But isn't the title one of the first things you write? Isn't it maybe the very first thing? I can't count the number of times I've had clients come to me with title ideas before we've even discussed the content. It's okay to put a tentative title on your manuscript when you start, but you should remain open to the idea that, like the narrative arc or even the theme, the title may well change, and for the same reasons. If the theme is what the book is really about, then the title is a way to reference what the theme is about. *Good-bye to All That* references innocence and a way of life that were lost because of World War I. *The Year of Magical Thinking* references the strange ways the human mind tries to make sense of tragedy. In neither case could the respective authors (Graves, Didion) have been able to conjure up these titles without first having nailed down the themes of their books. And since you're not one-hundred percent certain of your theme until you've finished (or are at least well on your way), I'd recommend waiting on the title. And besides, you might find some clever reference in the writing itself that might make a good title. So be patient. The title will come to you.

After your test readers, you're also going to want to run the manuscript past the people who are actually characters in it. This might be the scariest part so far, but if you've written about friends and family members, you owe it to them to let them see what you're about to put in print to reveal to the world, especially if not all the writing about them is complimentary. This doesn't mean you have to change something if they don't like it. You have a duty to your reader to be honest and you therefore ought to stick to your guns. On the other hand, you might run a passage about some incident past somebody who remembers the incident a little differently than how you remembered it, or who, perhaps, has an explanation for his actions that you'd never considered before. Maybe your take on his motivations was all wrong for instance. Your duty to be honest with your reader means looking at things from more than just your side. And keeping a loved one from being blindsided is just a good idea in and of itself, assuming, that is, that you care about maintaining your relationship with him or her after the book is published.

If there are characters in your book you don't care about maintaining a relationship with, or the relationship in question is broken anyway (the ex-boyfriend who used to beat you, or your estranged, alcoholic father), or there was no real relationship to begin with (the doctor who misdiagnosed you or the classmate who tried to strangle you), then you need to consider not just fairness and honesty; you need to consider the legal ramifications. Not that your best friend can't sue you, but if you've shown her the manuscript and she's okay with it, you're probably on pretty solid legal ground. The ex-boyfriend who's going to read about himself only after the book is published might be a different story.

Laws regarding defamation (*libel* in our case, since it's the written word, as opposed to *slander*, which is spoken) vary from state to state and you'll want to consult with a good attorney if you have any concerns about what you've written. But in general legal terms, defamation can occur when a *false statement* has been made about a person. Now, the false statement has to be presented as though it's a fact. The First Amendment allows you to present all the opinions you want to, even if they're wrong. Stating something as a fact is a different proposition.

Here's a simple example:

Ed was a cheater. He cheated on his taxes and he cheated on his wife.

This sure sounds like a statement of fact rather than opinion. But to be defamation, it has to be false. If it's been proven that Ed cheated on both his taxes and his wife, you're in the clear. If it hasn't been proven, you're opening up yourself to a lawsuit. You might want to do some rewriting, perhaps like this:

I could never be certain, but it sure seemed to me as though Ed was the cheating kind of guy. It would not have surprised me to learn that he cheated on his taxes and maybe even his wife.

This is your opinion and you have a constitutional right to voice it. In most states, to be defamation, the false statement has to also result in mental anguish or damages or harm to the person's reputation. If Ed suddenly starts getting audited because the IRS has read your book, or his business suffers because his customers have read what you've written about him, or his wife leaves him, he's got a good case (assuming you can't prove he really was a cheater).

Generally speaking, the false statement also has to be made with some degree of malice. If it's a line you tossed into the book, never imagining it would do any harm because, heck, everybody knows about Ed anyway, and you assumed (however incorrectly) that Ed would probably just laugh about it, you might be okay. No malice intended. All in good fun. But if its purpose was clearly to besmirch Ed, then he's going to have a good case, especially if he can show you've had it in for him for some time. But sometimes even an unintentional false statement can be considered libel if it's determined that you should have *reasonably* been able to anticipate that the statement would cause harm.

And don't think you can avoid any trouble by changing Ed's name to Fred. (Or even Alice, for that matter.) If a reader can make a reasonable guess that Fred is, in real life, Ed, then you can still be on the hook.

Bottom line: don't make a harmful statement about someone that you can't back up unless you make it clear that the statement is just your opinion. For more details, see an attorney.

Okay, so where are we? Well, we've written our manuscript; we've reviewed and rewritten our manuscript; we've put it away for a month, come back to it, and rewritten it again; we've lent it out to two objective test readers, taken those suggestions with which we've agreed and done some more rewriting; and we've shown certain passages about characters to the real-life people behind the characters, or else made sure we're on solid legal ground (or both).

Now what? Hang in there; we're almost to the promised land. All that's left is the polishing. But, oh, how important that is.

CHAPTER TEN

Polishing it Up

"When I get on a plane, I don't want a laid-back pilot. I want a pilot who is a control freak, who is paying attention to every single detail of his job."

—MICHAEL OVITZ

Let's talk about editing. As you've been writing and rewriting your manuscript, you've been editing it, too. In fact, editing by definition includes making modifications and making improvements. Rewriting is part of the editing process. But there are different levels of editing, with each level getting more and more detailed in nature.

Most books start out in need of *developmental editing*. This is where you're concerned about such issues as structure and plot. Is everything in the right order? Is there a way to infuse more dramatic tension? Has the theme been properly developed? Are the characters fleshed out sufficiently? The questions from chapters seven and eight more or less cover ground that belongs in the developmental-editing sphere. You can think of developmental editing as being concerned with the book in general.

The next level is *line editing*, which looks at the writing on a more specific level. Think of line editing as being concerned with the single paragraph or even the single sentence. You should be line editing as you go, but once your manuscript has made it past the gauntlet we described at the end of the last chapter, it wouldn't hurt to read it one more time with an eye toward these types of issues: redundancies, poor word choices, overused words, confusing sentences, extraneous description, unexpected changes in tone, forced dialogue, choppiness.

Here's a paragraph from the first draft of a client's book that eventually, through the process of line editing, I was able to improve:

> The incongruities of my father's life continually confused and perplexed me. I could remember him as a kind and decent man who loved his children and took pride in them. The whole world seemed to like and respect him. How could that be reconciled with what I knew about him?

Okay, not a bad paragraph. But for some reason the word "incongruities" stuck in my craw. It seemed a bit too fancy. I changed it to the simpler "contradictions." Then I decided to streamline "continually confused and perplexed me," which seemed awkward and also a bit redundant. Did I really need to say both "confused" *and* "perplexed"? Upon further review, "The whole world seemed to like and respect him" seemed a bit weak, and I wondered if maybe I could better exemplify just what was meant by that. Finally, I decided I didn't care for the rhetorical question. Plus, within the context of where this paragraph was in the narrative, it occurred to me that it needed to end more dramatically. After my editing, the paragraph looked like this:

> The contradictions of my father's life were inexplicable to me. I could remember him as a kind and decent man who loved his children and took pride in them. The world saw him as a friendly, generous, well-respected churchgoer and businessman. It was impossible to reconcile that man with the monstrous one who became transformed into a raging madman.[2]

Now, some of this, much of it actually, may be subjective. To some, incongruities may be preferable to contradictions. I didn't like the word in that spot, but that might just be me. Overall, however, I feel I made this paragraph stronger than it was and maybe a little more dramatic. Read through your manuscript and see if you can't find ways to make your writing stronger. Again, this is something you should be doing all along, but it's never too late to go through your manuscript one more time and pay attention to each paragraph and each sentence. Has everything been written as well as you can write it? Only you can answer this.

Eventually, you'll come to the *copyediting* part of the process. This is almost synonymous with proofreading, although within the publishing industry, proofreading technically refers to the final reading that is undertaken after the creation of the galley proof (hence "proof"-reading). The purpose of proofreading in this case is just to make sure everything will print as desired

---

[2] *Ellevie*, Marcelle Evie Guy, 2014 (Blue Fluke Media). With kind permission.

when the book finally hits the presses. But if you want to call it proofreading, that's fine by me.

At this point, we're really in the polishing stage. Copyediting is concerned with grammar, spelling, punctuation, capitalization, fonts, and other similar details that never seem all that important until you read something somebody wrote and come across a misspelled word or a grammatically-mutilated sentence that throws any credibility the writer might have had right down the trash chute. Don't let that happen to you. And don't assume you can do this adequately yourself. If you're like me, you probably haven't memorized all the rules of English grammar and punctuation, and even if you have, you're still not going to be able to read as carefully as you should to catch any mistakes you've made. Leave this task to a professional. There are several great proofreading services you can find online that will proofread your work for you and turn it around fairly quickly, and for just pennies per word. Find one and spend the money! It's well worth it.

And, by the way, you can delegate developmental editing and line editing to a professional, too. A good, experienced editor can prove invaluable, which is why even the masters use them. Even Ernest Hemingway had his Maxwell Perkins, perhaps the greatest editor of them all.

Just because you're going to delegate the proofreading, don't take that as license to ignore the rules. Great writing is often about the details, and you should get yourself in the habit of taking care of them. The self-discipline will help you be a more precise, more careful writer. At least maintain a general knowledge of the rules. Get yourself a copy of the *Chicago Manual of Style*. It's the rulebook. Well, one of them anyway. The other major source is the *AP Stylebook*.

I'm a *Chicago* man myself. There aren't a lot of differences, but a couple of them stick out to me. First and foremost is the way the two disagree on the use of a comma in a series. Chicago says to put a comma before the last item even if you're using "and." Hence: *I went to lunch with Kim, Todd, and Bernie.* AP says, unless it would otherwise be confusing, the last comma isn't necessary. *I went to lunch with Kim, Todd and Bernie.* But how do you always know what might or might not be confusing for a reader? Here, how about this sentence: *I went to lunch with Kim, my aunt and best friend.* Did I go to lunch with three people, or just one who is also my aunt and best friend? Here's an actually published "AP" sentence: *Among those interviewed were Merle Haggard's two ex-wives, Kris Kristofferson and Robert Duvall.* Kristofferson and Duvall probably would have appreciated that extra comma.

The other major difference is in how the two rulebooks handle numbers within text. Chicago says to spell out numbers up to and including one-hundred. AP says to spell them out only up to and including nine. Chicago: *seventy-seven.* AP: *77.* I happen to like words more than numbers, so I prefer Chicago.

In both cases, commas and numbers, AP is looking to save space. No surprise. AP stands for Associated Press, and the idea when they set up their rules was to write within the constraints of newspaper column width. An extra comma or a spelled-out number meant more valuable space was needed. You have no such constraints and so you might prefer Chicago like me. But whichever way you go, be consistent throughout.

One grammatical problem I see consistently with memoir writing has to do with verb tense, namely when to use *past perfect* tense as opposed to *simple past* tense. When you consider that memoirs are always written in past tense (we're writing about the past after all), the confusion is not surprising. When do you use *I traveled to Spain* versus *I had traveled to Spain*? This is a constant headache for many of my clients, but it's really not that difficult. Remember that your whole book is in the past. The purpose of past perfect is to describe something that's in the past of the past you're describing. Clear as mud? Here's an example:

> In Tampa, I met Wendell in a diner and we had coffee. Wendell worked as a police detective in New York, which is what gave him the experience to be a private investigator.

This makes it seem as if Wendell is still working in New York as a police detective. But what the writer really wanted to say (and I know because this was a real client of mine), was that Wendell worked in New York some time *before* these two people are sitting in a Tampa diner. Now Wendell's retired from the force and working as a private investigator. The problem is that the writer kept everything in simple past. But he's referencing something that happened before the diner. So he needs to use past perfect. Easy fix:

> In Tampa, I met Wendell in a diner and we had coffee. Wendell *had worked* as a police detective in New York, which is what *had given* him the experience to be a private investigator.

Just remember where—in time—you are. When you take a digression to a time before the time you're in (time as a detective in New York prior to the diner), the "perfect" tense to use is the past perfect tense.

For the sake of style, some rules are meant to be bent if not altogether broken. And some aren't really rules at all. Often I have to fight with a client who wonders why I would dare end a sentence with a preposition or start a sentence with a conjunction. And I have to explain that these ideas are antiquated and that the client's English teacher in junior high, no matter how well-intentioned, was wrong. There's no good reason not to end a sentence with a preposition. Listen to what H.W. Fowler, the dean of English scholars, had to say: "The power of saying *People worth talking to* instead of *People with whom it is worthwhile to talk* is not one to be lightly surrendered." I agree. We want to write sentences that are smooth and flowing, not tortured ones that are all twisted up just so we can adhere to some senseless "rule."

And not only do I sometimes start sentences with conjunctions, but I'll sometimes start whole paragraphs with them. Like this one. Why? Because I want to tie it into the previous paragraph and yet I want to slightly shift direction, or maybe emphasize the new point. But isn't that against a rule? And doesn't starting a sentence with "but" also break a rule? No. The "rule" is a complete myth. In fact, there never was one. At best, one could argue in favor of the "rule" for a piece of technical writing. Technical writing endeavors to come across as completely neutral and detached from any subjective point of view. Hence, stylistic choices aren't as effective for the purpose of the writing. But we're not writing technical papers.

Another rule that I advocate breaking if need be: the one that says a sentence must contain both a subject and a predicate. There are often good reasons to use an incomplete sentence.

Notice the one in the previous paragraph that reads: "Like this one." That's an incomplete sentence. I could have tied it to the previous sentence with a comma, but then my fear was that it would have gotten completely lost. I wanted it to stand out so that the reader could really get the point. I wanted emphasis, so I broke it off separately. It works alone perfectly well, even if it's not a true sentence in a technical sense.

Here's a generally accepted stylistic guideline that often annoys me: don't use the same word over and over. This is another one I often fight with my clients about. Yes, synonyms are important, but there are often good, practical reasons for repeating the same word. Here are a couple of sentences out of the introduction to this book:

> And each memoir I've worked on has been illuminating in its own unique way. I suppose that's not surprising; every memoir is unique because every life is unique.

I used "unique" three times in two sentences! Surely that's poor writing, revealing the author's deficient vocabulary. Well, let's see what happens when I open up my thesaurus:

> And each memoir I've worked on has been illuminating in its own unique way. I suppose that's not surprising; every memoir is distinctive because every life is inimitable.

Using "distinctive" and "inimitable" certainly shows I have an impressive vocabulary (or that I at least know what a thesaurus is), but something has now been lost with this passage. First, it's lost some flow. We've lost some symmetry, some balance. It's not parallel. Read both passages out loud and see if you don't agree.

More importantly, it's lost its power. The replacement words are very close in meaning, but we have different words available to us in the English language because we want *precision*. The replacement words don't mean exactly what "unique" means. I want to convey that memoirs and lives are *exactly* the same in one very important aspect: they're both *unique*. I don't want to say that one's distinctive while the other one is inimitable. That's close to what I want to say, but it's not what I want to say. Distinctive is not inimitable and neither means unique. I want to say that lives are unique and that memoirs are unique, too. They both share this one specific characteristic. And saying it the way I said it is where the passage gets its power. It's a question of context. Always think of the context.

Never forget the goal of writing is to communicate effectively. If there's a way to better do that, but that way might require breaking a rule or a guideline, go right ahead. In the end, grammar is a tool for our use. We're not here to serve it. It's here to serve us.

CHAPTER ELEVEN

Traditional Publishing

"I have to declare in all candor that no one interested in being published in our time can afford to be so naive as to believe that a book will make it merely because it's good."

—RICHARD CURTIS

Believe it or not, someday your book is going to be finished. It will have been written and rewritten, line edited and copyedited. This is simultaneously a satisfying moment and a scary one. Scary, because what are you going to *do* with it? Let's run over the options. There are three: you can do nothing, you can try to interest a publisher, or you can self-publish.

Whatever you do, don't do nothing. Maybe you have some doubts about your finished product. Maybe you think your memoir is no good. Maybe you think nobody would be interested in reading it. Join the club. We all have these thoughts and they're all very understandable reasons for wanting to shove the manuscript deep into a drawer somewhere. And they're all insufficient. You've come too far and worked too hard. Make something out of all of that work. Allow the world (or at least friends and family) to share in your life experiences. If just one person somewhere (including a potential great-great-great grandchild sometime in the distant future) gets something out of it, then you owe it to that person to make the book available.

So should you try to interest a publishing house, or should you self-publish your book? Here's the hard truth: these days, it's virtually impossible to publish a book through a traditional publishing house like HarperCollins, Penguin Random House, or Simon and Schuster. Maybe it's not *technically* impossible, but the odds are so slim as to render the possibilities merely theoretical for most people. It greatly helps if you know somebody in the publishing industry—an editor who works for a publisher, perhaps, or a literary agent with whom you have a personal relationship. Publishing is like every other industry. (And why wouldn't it be?) Many times, it's *who* you know. Connections matter. Failing any connections, it helps if you're already famous, thus guaranteeing a lot of book sales. These seem to be the only people getting published nowadays by the big publishing companies—people with connections and people whose names are already well known. Those in the mainstream publishing industry might try to refute this, but they're not helped by the statistics. Less than one-half of one percent of manuscripts submitted to the mainstream publishing houses by people outside these two groups is accepted for publication.[3]

---

[3] Numbers are hard to come by, but this is a common statistic I've seen that has been confirmed for me by the best estimates of several industry insiders. I have no reason to doubt it.

It's hard to blame the publishers for this once you understand the state of their industry. The traditional book publishing business is in a freefall. It all began unraveling years ago when the so-called big-box bookstores like Barnes & Noble and Borders and Books-a-Million came along. With tremendous buying power, these huge chains were able to dictate to the publishers the wholesale pricing terms that they'd accept in order to carry the publishers' books in their stores, which were typically much lower than in the old days. But if you were a publisher and you wanted to sell your book through, say, Barnes & Noble, you had to take what they'd give you. In turn, Barnes & Noble would pass along their savings to their customers. It was the Walmart business model. The price of books came down. This was great news for the consumer but bad news for publishers and authors (not to mention the small mom-and-pop bookstores that could no longer compete and were forced out of business).

Then things became even worse for the profitability of the publishers. A little phenomenon called the Internet came along, and with it, an upstart company called Amazon. They could sell the books even cheaper than the big-box stores because they didn't have the overhead of actual "stores." And when eBooks came along, more profit got sucked out of the industry as prices came down further. The big-box stores got out-big-boxed (a little karma the out-of-business mom-and-pop stores could no doubt appreciate). Borders went under, and today most people I know go to Barnes & Noble and Books-a-Million for the coffee and free Wi-Fi. (Both have an online presence, but nothing approaching Amazon's online domination.)

Meanwhile, many publishers went out of business, several merged, everyone downsized or streamlined, and nobody left will touch a book unless there's a guaranteed market for it. How does a publisher know in advance there will be a sure market for a book? They work only with authors who have already built large audiences for their books even before their books are finished. (Sometimes even having a connection to a publisher won't help if you're unknown to the world.) In the trade, this is called having a "platform." It's an industry buzzword that essentially means the author has a following. He or she has some degree of fame. If an author has a big enough platform, the publisher knows that if the book hits the shelves this morning, tons of people will buy it by this afternoon.

Alas, that counts the vast majority of us out.

Having said all that, if you still want to try getting published in the traditional way, far be it from me to try to talk you out of it (at least beyond what I've said so far about the matter). But you'll need to know a few things about the process. First, you'll have to find a literary agent. Publishers rarely work directly with authors (unless those authors have names like Stephen King or John Grisham or J.K. Rowling). For most authors, publishers prefer to work with agents and the agents end up acting as the publishers' gatekeepers. Most agents work in New York City where the major publishing houses are, and they all have connections with the editors of those houses. (A lot of agents actually got their starts working for the publishers in their editing departments before they went out on their own.) You'll need to be represented by an agent, but that's okay because an agent will work on your behalf to make sure you're getting the best deal. He or she will become your advocate, which is a good thing to have if you're negotiating with, say, Simon and Schuster.

Agents don't take anything up front. Instead, they typically take fifteen percent of the book's eventual royalties. They only get paid when you get paid. Consequently, they don't spend a lot of time working with books they don't think will sell. So, if you secure the services of an agent, you can be fairly certain they'll find a publisher. With a few exceptions, I've always found agents to be a supercilious bunch, a bit intoxicated on the power of being the keepers of the gate. But if you want to get your book published in the mainstream, you're just going to have to swallow your pride and work with them.

How do you find an agent? There are several good online sources I would recommend including LiteraryMarketplace.com, PublishersMarketplace.com, AgentQuery.com, QueryTracker.net, and WritersMarket.com. These sites all have searchable databases, making it easy to find lists of agents who represent your particular genre (memoir).

All the agents have websites, so once you identify them from your search, you can visit their sites to find out exactly how they like to be approached. A note of caution: there are some unscrupulous agents out there. Never deal with an agent who charges a reading fee. That's a big red flag. And watch out for agents who read your work and make big promises about getting it published if you just spend a few thousand dollars with them so that they can edit the book for you before the search for a publisher begins. That's another big red flag. Make sure the agent is a member of the AAR (Association of Authors' Representatives). They have a "Canon of Ethics" they follow. You can find more information about the association, including a searchable database, at aaronline.org.

For most agents, the process works more or less like so: you send a query letter, typically by email. An effective query letter (quickly) gets the agent's attention, sums up the book, tells a little about you, and basically gives the agent a reason to want to look further into your book. It's a written sales pitch. You have one chance with each agent, so your query letter better be perfect. There are a lot of tips online about writing query letters, so do a little research.

Be ready for a *lot* of rejection at this point. If they're not interested, most agents won't even bother with a reply. This might seem unprofessional, but the fact is, these people get hundreds of queries a month and it's just not practical for them to take the time to send everyone a personalized rejection letter or email. The nicer ones make use of a form letter of some description, and these typically read like so: "Dear author, thanks for thinking of the XYZ Literary Agency. Your story, although promising, doesn't fit in with the kinds of books we're looking to represent these days. Other agencies may feel differently, however, so best of luck in your continued pursuit of agency representation." (I have enough of these to paper my bathroom.) Rarely, if ever, will an agent give you the reason why they declined your offering, so if you're looking for constructive criticism, you'll need to look elsewhere. Don't waste your time wondering what it was specifically that the agent didn't like. And never, ever, take a rejection personally.

If, on receiving your query, an agent is interested in looking further, he or she will typically ask to see either the completed manuscript (don't send a query if your book isn't finished) or a book proposal. A book proposal normally includes a summary of the book, information about the author (you!), details about your platform, market information (who the audience is, how best to reach them, etc.), comparisons with similar books from the genre, a detailed outline, and the first few chapters of your manuscript. Essentially, the proposal lays out a case for the book.

Annoyingly, there doesn't seem to be a consensus among agents on the necessity of a book proposal for memoir. A book proposal has a clear role in the nonfiction realm. Nonfiction is often more about the author than the content, especially nonfiction books like how-to books or books on politics or current events. What, in these cases, gives the author the expertise necessary to write the book? This is what a proposal needs to answer. Fiction, on the other hand, is judged more on the story itself. Who cares what the writer's background or credentials are if the story is compelling and marketable? (Of course, they'll still care about the size of your potential audience.) Memoir falls somewhere in between. A memoir is true, so it's nonfiction, but it reads more like a novel, so in that sense it's comparable more to fiction than a how-to book. Consequently, some agents want to see a proposal, some don't.

To be ready for whatever an agent asks for if you get past the query stage, it's probably a good idea to prepare a proposal, just to make sure you have all your bases covered. Since this isn't a book on how to write the perfect book proposal, I might recommend another book for this purpose: *Write the Perfect Book Proposal* (of course), by Jeff and Deborah Herman (Turner, third ed., 2016). The authors are literary agents themselves and a lot of agents recommend this book. Since they're the people you're trying to impress, I would definitely use it.

Finally, if the agent likes the proposal, they'll ask to see the manuscript. Rejection at this point stings a little more. When a query or a proposal gets rejected, the agent might just dislike the idea of the book, not the book itself. Or maybe she's not sold on the size of your platform. When the manuscript gets rejected, it may well mean that she doesn't like the writing. Ouch. Most agents will provide some feedback at this stage, however small it might be. They've taken the time to read some or most of your manuscript, and so they've formed an opinion that they will often share. If not, I believe you're well within your rights to reply with a simple, courteous request for feedback. "Thanks for your consideration, Ms. Cerberus. Out of curiosity, and a deep desire to make my manuscript the best it can be, I wonder if I might be able to prevail upon you to briefly share with me your reasons for declining the manuscript. Anything you can offer would be appreciated." You have nothing to lose at this point by asking. Just make sure there's nothing at all defensive in your tone. If you hear back, great. Maybe she sends back with some criticism you can use. Otherwise, just move on.

While all of this search for an agent is underway, and even before (maybe even *way* before), you need to be building that platform the publisher is going to want to see. You need to build an audience for the book. In this day and age, that means doing lots of social media stuff: Facebook, Twitter, LinkedIn, Instagram, Snapchat, YouTube, etc. Build a website for the book and drive people there. Blog. Do search engine optimization. Post excerpts of your book. *Create a following.* Outside the online world, make public speaking appearances, write articles, send out press releases, try to get yourself interviewed by your local newspaper. Hire a public relations person to help you, somebody skilled in social media as well as the more traditional avenues of generating publicity—and somebody who understands book promotion in particular. Sure, all of this can be expensive and time-consuming. But remember, if you're not well known, the publishing houses probably won't take a chance on you, *no matter how good your manuscript is.*

One final thing to try is querying the smaller publishing houses. Outside the big ones in New York, there are many small publishers who typically specialize in certain genres. Many of them will take queries directly from authors—no agent required. These are not to be confused with "imprints." Imprints are branches of the big guys. Flatiron Books sounds like a nice, small, approachable publisher, doesn't it? Probably open-minded and willing to consider a new author. Alas, Flatiron is an imprint of Macmillan, a big guy. (Macmillan itself, interestingly, is a subsidiary of an even bigger conglomerate called Holtzbrinck Publishing Group.) What you want to find are *indie* publishing houses—independent publishers. As with agents, databases exist online. Don't mistake "vanity" publishers for indie publishers. We'll talk more about the vanity presses in the next chapter. These are publishing houses that charge money to publish your book. That's not traditional publishing.

Indie publishers are approached the same way agents are approached: query, proposal, manuscript. They're generally a little more open-minded than the big publishing companies, as long as your book fits within the scope of books for which they specialize. But they're still going to want to see a platform. And the downside is that they're probably not going to spend the same kind of money to market your book as what the big guys would spend, simply because their budgets are smaller. Then again, if you have a big enough platform, the marketing might take care of itself.

Any way you slice it, it's an uphill climb. Without a huge platform and/or some kind of connection, the chances of getting published by the mainstream literary industry are about the same as winning the lottery. Or getting struck by lightning. Or getting struck by lightning *while* winning the lottery. But for those brave enough to try, best of luck. Stay positive and keep at it. For the rest of us, there's another way: the way of the future.

CHAPTER TWELVE

Self-Publishing:
The Twenty-First Century Way

*"I enjoy self-publishing and sending publishers
rejection letters. They're like, 'Who is this guy?'
And I'm like, 'The end of your industry.'"*

—RYAN LILLY

If you're not keen on putting yourself through the wringer that
is the mainstream publishing world today (and who could blame
you?), you might want to consider the business model of the
future: *self-publishing.* Yes, there will always be big publishing houses willing to spend money on sure-things like Dean
Koontz's next novel, but if you're a relative unknown with no
connections to the trade, you can do what a lot of smart authors
are doing these days (even some with large platforms, and even
some who have been published by the big guys before): you can
take matters into your own hands and bypass the publisher
middleman.

101

More and more, writers are doing this—with print books and increasingly with eBooks. And they're keeping the profits for themselves. Make no mistake: if you can sell your book to a mainstream publisher, you should. If HarperCollins is interested in your book and willing to advertise it and make sure it gets shelf space in bookstores all over the world, and you're going to get reviewed by the *New York Times Book Review*, you're going to sell a lot more copies than if you self-publish. But if your book doesn't end up in that special one-half of one percent that mainstream publishers accept, self-publishing is a terrific, potentially profitable alternative. Besides, even if you make it into that privileged space, there's no guarantee that the publisher will be willing to make a huge financial commitment to advertise your book. And even if they do, you're going to need a lot of sales to make any real money at the royalty rate of eight percent or even less that publishers are paying today (minus your agent's fee!).

So how do you self-publish your book? Well, you can do all or most of it yourself—true self-publishing—or you can pay to have someone else do it for you, a "subsidy" or "vanity" publisher.

Let's start with the do-it-yourself approach. In this case, you become the publisher of your book. Now, if you're thinking of just creating a book for family and friends and not making it available for sale, you need do nothing but contact a book manufacturing company. Many large print shops have the capability of printing books. They can even help with the cover design and formatting of the book. Easy enough.

If, on the other hand, you want to make your book available to retail booksellers so that the world can buy it, you'll need to make use of a wholesaler-distributor. Not surprisingly, that's where the retailers get their books. The two largest book wholesalers in the United States are Ingram and Baker & Taylor.

Ingram, through its IngramSpark arm (ingramspark.com), provides print-on-demand (POD) services for publishers. POD is becoming very popular because you don't have to pay to print any of your books until someone actually orders one. In the old days, you had to pay up front for a print run of a whole slew of books at once, and then you needed to store them someplace until buyers could be found. With today's new digital printing technology, you can have just one book printed at a time. Or a thousand. However many you need. Someone finds your book on Amazon (where IngramSpark has made it available), he or she orders it, and IngramSpark prints and ships it to them. Easy peasy.

Since IngramSpark is a wholesaler, they'll require a wholesale price from you, generally a fifty-five percent discount from whatever retail price you've placed on the book. Essentially, you're selling it to them at a discount so they can sell it to the retailers.

Keep in mind that working with IngramSpark as your wholesaler doesn't mean they're going to distribute your book to every Barnes & Noble so that Barnes & Noble can stock them on their shelves. The mainstream publishers still have the upper hand where shelf space is concerned. But it does mean that somebody can walk into a Barnes & Noble and at least *order* your book. Or they can go to Barnes & Noble online and order it.

You can also run your book through CreateSpace, an Amazon company. It's POD as well, but since it's an Amazon company, you probably won't be able to sell your book through other retail outlets.

Working with IngramSpark (or CreateSpace) starts by simply setting up an account with them. Then you need to make your manuscript ready for them to print and make available to the buying public. That means your manuscript needs to be formatted properly. It needs to look like a book! It needs an eye-catching cover design, the correct placement of the barcode (more on this in a bit), the proper use of font and spacing, page numbering, proper insertion of illustrations, etc. Don't skimp on any of this. Hire a professional graphic designer and do it right. IngramSpark and CreateSpace have templates available, but you might consider finding a company that specializes in book formatting. (One in particular that I like is Wordzworth. com.)

Don't forget to include all of the appropriate "front" and "back matter" for the book: the copyright page, a title page, an acknowledgements page, a dedication page, a table of contents (if you feel it's necessary), an "About the Author" page, etc. Don't reinvent the wheel—find a book that's similar to the one you've written and use it as a guide.

Speaking of the copyright page, a note about copyrighting your book: the law recognizes that a work is automatically copyrighted the moment it's created. If you create something new and put your name on it, it belongs to you. Nobody can legally take it. No registration is necessary. Just the same, you'll want to provide notice of your rights in the book by putting: Copyright © by "Your Name," "Year," All Rights Reserved. (See the copyright page at the front of this book.) If you want more protection, and public notice of your copyright, or if you just want a little more proof that the work is yours in case you ever have to file a lawsuit because someone has plagiarized your book, you'll want to register your copyright, something easily done by visiting the U.S. Copyright Office online at copyright.gov.

For your book to be sold retail, you'll need an ISBN—an International Standard Book Number. These ten- and thirteen-digit numbers are part of the universal numbering system that identifies each and every book for sale. You can purchase an ISBN from R.R. Bowker, LLC, the official United States ISBN Agency (go to myidentifiers.com). These numbers also come with barcodes. This tells a bookstore how much to sell the book for. You'll need to decide on the price of your printed book before you buy a barcode for it. Every version of your book—the print version (both the hardcover and soft cover versions if you're going to have both), the eBook version, and future editions—needs a separate ISBN. And if you decide down the road to change the price, you'll have to buy a new ISBN and, if it's a printed book, a new barcode. (For an example of a barcode with an ISBN, just look on the back cover of any book, including this one if you're reading the printed version of it.) If you want your book in libraries, you'll also need a Library of Congress Control Number (LCCN), which you can acquire for free by going to the Library of Congress website and opening an account for your book (loc.gov/publish/pcn).

A point to note: the numbers correspond to the name of the publisher. That means that if someone searches for your book by the ISBN or the LCCN, they'll come across your name. That's the name that will show up on Amazon, too. Unfortunately, that makes it clear that the book is self-published, and self-published books often don't get the same amount of respect as books published by the big publishing houses. So, a little marketing tip: start your own publishing business with its own creative name. A name like "Greatbooks Press" will give your book a little added credibility. How hard is it to set up a publishing company? As hard as filing a fictitious name with your state, something that can typically be done online. Check with your state government to find out the specific requirements and start selling your book through the name of your own bona fide publishing company. This, by the way, is the name in which you'll set up your IngramSpark or CreateSpace account.

You might even decide to design a little logo to go with your name. Use the name and logo on the copyright page and even the spine of the book. You'll give your book an even more professional look, and, contrary to the old saw, people often do judge books by their covers.

What about eBooks? To turn your manuscript into an eBook, you'll need to have it formatted so that it can be made available for e-readers (like Kindle). There is software available to help you do this, or, if you're not particularly computer literate, you can always hire someone to convert it for you.

That's the nuts and bolts. If you want a more thorough discussion of self-publishing, I recommend *Successful Self-Publishing: How to Self-Publish and Market Your Book* by Joanna Penn (Joanna Penn, 2015). It's a short, easy read and full of great ideas.

Now, what if you just don't want to mess with doing all of this work yourself? As you might suspect, there are companies that will take care of all of these details for you. They'll design your cover, format your book, produce e-versions, register your copyright, secure the ISBN, barcodes, and LCCN, as well as print your book, market it, and distribute it. Their name, not yours, will be listed in the book as the publisher.

These so-called subsidy or vanity presses can be expensive. Often, they also pay royalties, as opposed to net profits, and although the royalty percentages are normally higher than what mainstream publishers pay, they may not be higher by much. Some subsidy presses even acquire the copyright of the book for themselves, obtaining the full rights from the author as a condition of marketing the book! Needless to say, you should *never* give your copyright away. Some subsidy publishers are excellent, consulting with you and willing to work with you closely every step of the way. Some are outright scams, taking a fee upfront to print the book and then not following through on the promised marketing of the book. If you're thinking of using a subsidy press, do your homework. Search around the Internet to see what their customers have to say about them. Plug their name into Google and enter the word "scam" behind it and see what pops up. See if they're listed with the Better Business Bureau and find out what their rating is. Read reviews. You know the drill.

Okay, so what happens once your book has been successfully self-published, either by yourself or with the help of a subsidy press? Well, it's not going to sell itself. Remember that platform we talked about? You'll still need to build one. Publishing a book is not the same as selling a book, or even marketing a book. You've had it printed and made available, but people still need to know to look for it in the first place. They need to know it exists. Just because it's on Amazon doesn't mean people will find it. Keep working on that platform. Do the social marketing, send out press releases, talk to your local bookstore about doing a signing. Get creative. Work it!

As the mainstream publishing industry continues its freefall, producing caution if not downright fear in publishers and literary agents alike, more and more people are taking advantage of the new opportunities the Internet has made available for self-publishing books. Some authors will be more successful than others. With the right planning, the right promotional efforts, and (of course) the right book, anything can happen. Heck, you might sell enough copies that some literary agent or publishing house someplace takes notice and contacts *you*. Then you get to be the gatekeeper. How sweet would that be?

Final Thoughts

"Beware of advice—even this."

—CARL SANDBURG

I hope your book is successful. I hope you get published by Random House and sell a million copies. Or that you self-publish and still sell a ton of books. Or that at least your family and friends read it and get something valuable out of it. More than anything, I hope you just finish it.

The world is filled with aspiring writers. Don't be one of those. Be a writer. That means writing and not talking about writing or wishing you were a writer. How do you know when you're a writer? When you're famous? When you're published? I would say you're a writer when you actually write, but also when you finish whatever it is you're writing. And finish it well.

I know this isn't easy to do. Finishing a project well, taking it through the process I've described in this little book, is a monumental task. I can't count the number of books I've written that frustrated me to the point where I wanted to quit. I couldn't get the story right. I lost track of the theme. The characters weren't coming out the way they should have. There were too many rewrites needed, even wholesale restructuring. Everything seemed wrong. Honestly, there have been times when the only thing that kept me going was the contract I'd signed with the client. I was legally obligated to finish the book or else surrender the fee. And when the mortgage is due, that's not really a very smart option. So I kept going.

I like to think I'd have finished the projects anyway. In addition to the legal obligation, I felt a moral obligation. These people were counting on me to navigate them through the difficult process of writing about their lives. If I got us off course, it was up to me to get us back on track. "We're not lost," says a character in the film *Meek's Cutoff.* "We're just finding our way." That's really what any journey is about, and writing a memoir is nothing less than a journey. Just keep finding your way.

So in the worst of it, when you find yourself frustrated beyond your desire to continue, power through as if you're being paid for it, because the pay *will* come. Maybe not financially, but at least in the satisfaction of completing the journey. And in the satisfaction of perhaps gaining some self-awareness, of learning something about yourself by dissecting your life.

And perhaps mostly in the satisfaction of knowing, when you're finished, that now you're a writer.

Acknowledgments

This book could not have been made possible without each and every one of my wonderful clients. You are why I write. Thank you all for having allowed me the extraordinary opportunity to help you tell your stories.

About the Author

Jerry Payne is an award-winning ghostwriter. He has written or edited over two dozen memoirs for a wide range of clients, each story as unique as the life from which it was drawn.

Payne lives in St. Petersburg, Florida spending the majority of his time either working on clients' projects, or cruising the bay on *Pilar*, his beloved sailboat.

Connect with Jerry Payne at
www.YourConfidentialGhostwriter.com